CELEBRATING
HUMANITY

Also by Jack Bloomfield:

~~~~~~

One Planet United; *The Problem, The Solution and A Plan of Action*

CELEBRATING HUMANITY

Reflections, Insights and Hope for a United Planet

JACK BLOOMFIELD

Author of *ONE PLANET UNITED*

iUniverse, Inc.
New York Lincoln Shanghai

Celebrating Humanity
Reflections, Insights and Hope for a United Planet

iUniverse books may be ordered through booksellers or by contacting:

iUniverse
2021 Pine Lake Road, Suite 100
Lincoln, NE 68512
www.iuniverse.com
1-800-Authors (1-800-288-4677)

Because of the dynamic nature of the Internet, any Web addresses
or links contained in this book may have changed
since publication and may no longer be valid.

ISBN: 978-0-595-48798-1 (pbk)
ISBN: 978-0-595-60848-5 (ebk)

Printed in the United States of America

Should it Ever Really Matter?

We are a divided people; We are a divided planet.
What would it take to see a world transformed
into a place where when we see one another,
our first thought is; this is my brother;
this is my sister; this is a member of my family?

Should it ever really matter
What country we were born in? The color of our skin?
What religion we were born into or today choose to practice?
Who we vote for or what sexual orientation we happen to be?
Should it ever really matter what side of town we live on?

If we desire connection, unity, and peace with all people,
let us begin by knowing that there is only one thing
that should bind us together;
That is;
that we all have a beating heart and this reality
is all that is necessary to ultimately,
connect us all.

Contents

Acknowledgements

To my sister-in-law Karen. Your words of encouragement were the inspiration that brought this book into being.

To my wife Janice who has been my friend and partner for over 30 years. Your love and encouragement keep me listening to the voice of inspiration that keeps pushing me along.

To my son Matt and my daughter Jaime. My love for you both has no words. It can only be experienced through our feelings of love for one another which I feel each and every time we are together as well as when we are apart.

To Ruben Cueto, then editor of the Coral Springs Forum who read my first two trial columns and believed that they had enough value to make me an official "columnist."

To God, who comes to me more and more as a mystery these days but never the less, is as real as ever.

~~~~~~

In memory of Pat R. Turro

Preface

This book came into being as a result of a phone call. A few years ago, I was speaking with my sister-in-law and she was commenting on how much she loved my last column that she had received via email. She said to me, "I want you to know that I am saving all of your columns. I'm keeping them in a binder for Heather so when she comes of age, she'll be able to read them. It is my hope that she will grow up to live in a world in which you are writing about."

I was very moved by her affirming comments. Heather is her daughter and my very special niece who was 2 years old at the time of our conversation. My ensuing response was, "Maybe one day, I'll put them all together in a book so they'll be easier for her to read."

Let me digress for just a minute. Back in 2003, I approached the local newspaper in my town requesting that I be able to submit a couple of samples for a column that I felt inspired to write. It was my hope that the editor would find them inspirational and insightful enough that I would be able to write a column each week and become a regular writer for the paper. It was called The Coral Springs Forum and it was a small local newspaper of the town I resided in called Coral Springs in Florida. It was full of local news, sporting events, and upcoming special events such as art shows, concerts etc. Advertisements filled at least half of the paper hoping to get the attention of the 125,000 people who lived in Coral Springs.

For many years, I had always been someone who, when angered or frustrated, would write a "letter to the editor." Most times, my letters never made it into print. Although I would be discouraged that most often no one was able to read my thoughts on a particular matter, I remember that I always felt better just for writing them down and getting them off my chest.

The idea I had for a column came from my increased awareness of how most human beings live their day to day lives in a world of division. Divided by race, religious beliefs, political affiliation, age, class status and more. I was becoming more and more aware that we are a divided planet and a divided people and I wanted to have an outlet to share my thoughts, insights and feelings.

Around this time, I had become a member of The Coral Springs Interfaith Committee. This was one of many committees that were part of the Coral Springs Multi-Cultural Advisory committee. The Multi-Cultural Advisory Committee was created to educate the citizens of Coral Springs on issues of diversity among many other initiatives that make a city stronger and friendlier. The Interfaith Committee was responsible for hosting city events that embraced the diversity of religion. Their initiative was to plan events that would bring different religious groups together to try to gain a deeper understanding and respect for one another.

The year before I joined this committee, I had attended one of the annual events that they hosted called "The National Day of Prayer" Celebration. This is an annual day of recognition and a call for all Americans to pray for our nation and its leaders. NDP was first signed into law in 1952 by President Harry S. Truman and later amended in 1988 and signed by President Ronald Reagan to be held annually on the first Thursday of May.

Coral Springs had been celebrating this event for many years. In most cities and towns across the U.S., this celebration is conducted in honor of the National Day of Prayer, but from the beginning, I learned that the City of Coral Springs decided to create a different atmosphere. You see, the vast majority of theses celebrations across the United States are "Christian" celebrations which most often only include different denominations of Christianity to come together to pray. In Coral Springs, the invitation is open to all faith traditions and expressions. ALL people of faith and every house of worship and religious congregation are invited and encouraged to participate.

I found another thing fascinating regarding the format of the program designed by the city. The children are invited to share the prayer for peace while an adult representative is encouraged to stand next to them for support. As I sat and took in the experience for the first time, I was touched and often moved to tears as Muslim children, Buddhist children, Bahai' children, Jewish children, Christian children, Hindu children, and Native American Indian children came forward lifting up the innocent prayers that only can come from the hearts of the young and mostly innocent. You could tell that a few of the prayers that were read by the children were more than likely penned by an adult. All the same, by having a format where the children of all different faith communities came forward, I experienced a sense of religious unity that I had never known until this point.

At the completion of the program, I went to look for the chairperson to thank her and tell her what a beautiful event her committee had put together. She was very grateful for my comments. So much so I guess, because she asked me if I wanted to join the committee for the same event the following year. I said I would be honored and gave her my commitment to help.

As the result of my work on this committee, my love for interfaith relations began to grow deeper and deeper. I was also gaining a deeper awareness of the reality that religious unity was often times non-existent among people of different faiths. I was witnessing religious division more and more in the world but also in my hometown as well. As a member of the committee, I would offer to pay a personal visit to any congregations that would not respond to our invitations to participate in the NDP celebration only to hear on more than one occasion, "We do not participate in events such as this where people are worshipping false Gods." My day to day discussions with many other people of faith pointed out to me that there was an abundance of religious exclusivism and division that was alive and well.

At this same time, the world had recently experienced two tragic events that gripped the hearts of us all. In April of 1999 at Columbine High School in Colorado, twelve innocent students and one very brave teacher were tragically murdered by two unstable teenagers bent on destruction. Then came the devastating day of September 11, 2001 where the world was changed forever in a few brief minutes.

Tragic incidents as these were triggering the insides of many people to create deeper divides. One class against another, one religion against another, one race or culture against another. On the other hand, I was also keenly aware that these same events that could trigger such hatred and divide were also responsible for a greater amount of unity among many groups. I thought, how can this be? How can Religion bring so much division on one hand and on the other hand be the catalyst for unity? How can a devastating event such as the horrors of 9-11 cause rage and anger against another group while at the same time, with others, bringing human hearts together in a deep call to unity?

These were the questions I was asking myself that prompted me to write the first two columns that I brought to the Coral Springs Forum on that initial day. I had been thinking of a title for the column and the one that came to me was One Planet United. My goal was to expose how prejudice, intolerance and fear were at the core of so much of the division among people in our world today while at the same time, try to offer some insights and solutions for healing. My objective in each column was to remind the reader that we need to come to a higher consciousness in relating to others if we want to live in a world of understanding and mutual respect. It was, and is today, my hope that one day soon we will live in a world where the term "Love your neighbor" is a reality for us all.

In a unique format of short stories, insights and observations, this book is a collection of some of my columns that I have written over the past four years. It is my hope that my writings inspire you to reach a higher place of consciousness, that you will come to see ALL people as members of your same human family and that you will, as I do, celebrate humanity each and every day.

Jack Bloomfield
Coral Springs, Florida

Introduction

When it comes to celebrations, the list we currently participate in is quite extensive. We celebrate birthdays, anniversaries, special days such as St. Patrick's Day and Valentines Day, and major religious holidays that include Christmas, Easter, Hanukkah and Ramadan. We celebrate the birth of the U.S.A on the 4th of July with fireworks displays that often take our breath away. Many cities around the country hold cultural and regional celebrations in honor of a particular ethnicity or lifestyle. In each celebration, there is one thing missing. Someone is usually left out. Not on purpose. It's just because the occasion doesn't fit.

Of course, not everyone was born on the same day (birthdays), married on the same day (anniversaries), is Irish (St. Patrick's Day) or in a love relationship (Valentines Day). Some folks don't practice a particular religion or are not patriots or even Americans for that matter. But all people on the planet share one thing in common that we can all celebrate; that being, we are all human beings which is the one label that contains no division, and where no one can be excluded.

In the following pages, you will be absorbed in an assortment of short readings that in the end, always call for us to celebrate humanity. It is a call to cherish humanity, embrace humanity and to see *all* people as our brothers and sisters and members of our own family.

It is my hope that as you read this book you will be moved to be one who will ultimately join me in the celebration of humanity. I assure you that if you begin to look at every person you come in contact with as a member of your own human family, you'll find cause for a very special celebration! Peace out.

About the One Planet United Column

Writing a column is a great way to express whatever you feel on a given subject but it comes with the guarantee that not everyone will agree with you. I always invite readers of the One Planet United column to drop me an email and share their thoughts and feelings about the topics that I write about. Many of the responses that come back to me are uplifting and full of encouragement, but many are vehemently opposed to my commentary.

You might have guessed that the most passionate responses I receive from readers, both positive and negative, are when the subject addresses religion or politics. Aren't these the two subjects that everyone says you should never talk about? From my experience with the One Planet United column, there is certainly a lot of truth in that belief.

One column I wrote was on the subject of patriotism and I stated that it was my belief that patriotism, for some, has turned to nationalism. I invited the readers to investigate their strong feelings of patriotism and whether it included a distaste or worse yet, a hatred for anyone who was not American? I also suggested that the phrase "United We Stand" that appears on many t-shirts and bumper stickers could be seen as divisive because there is usually an American flag pictured directly next to the phrase. I said I felt it would be better if we inserted a globe along side the phrase "United We Stand." It would then be an inclusive phrase and symbol for all human beings, Americans as well as non-Americans. I received one email after this column from a staunch "patriot" who told me I should move to another country.

Another column I wrote was aimed at bringing the fundamentalist beliefs of many Christians to light showing the many ways that I believe they are making the religion of Christianity into an "Us and Them" club built on exclusivism. I said that I'm not sure that their approach was what Jesus had in mind. I had mentioned that even though I had been a follower of Jesus Christ all of my adult life, I disagreed with the belief that only Christians are following the one true path to God. I said that I honored all people of faith and believed that the superiority claims of many Christians was a great catalyst for division in the world. I was told by one reader that I should not call myself a Christian if I believe that all people are equal in the eyes of God.

My columns touch on many different subjects but the main thesis is two-fold. First, my writings are aimed at exposing the many different ways that human beings divide themselves from one another and secondly to try to inspire my readers to come to a higher place of consciousness by seeing all people as equals sharing this magnificent journey called life.

CHAPTER 1

Humanity

The Human Label

One night a man had a dream. Actually it was more like a nightmare. He dreamed that he was going up and down the aisles in his local supermarket in search of the items on his weekly shopping list, but something was terribly wrong. Every can and every box on all of the shelves had no labels on them. He was totally lost and didn't know which products to choose. He wanted to by a can of corn but all the cans looked the same. In the next aisle, he was looking to buy oatmeal but all the boxes were blank on the outside so he could not make a choice. He thought maybe his only option was to make a guess and take his chances when he got home that he had made the right choice.

I never got to hear how this man's dream ended, but it made me think that in a lot of situations, labels are vitally important so we can know what's inside. If we were purchasing light bulbs, it's would be very frustrating if we could not identify the wattage of the bulbs. I'd be very discouraged if I returned home with a carton of lemonade when what I was looking for was orange juice. Labels are extremely necessary when it comes to picking the correct products in a store but what about labels when we use them to identify people or groups of people?

Each day as I have conversations with individuals, listen to the radio in my car or read the newspaper, I can't help but notice how often labels are used to identify people. Any of these sound familiar? Black, white, non-white, Arab, middle easterner, Indian, Christian, Jew, Muslim, communist, atheist, conservative, liberal, progressive, elitist, fundamentalist, communist, the right, the far right, the left, the far left, gay, anti-gay, humanist, creationist, secularist, the elite media ad infinitum. Maybe a new label that could be used could be to call someone a "labelist." That would be someone who identifies individuals or groups by using labels.

So is there anything wrong with using labels when it comes to identifying a person or group of people? From what I can tell the answer is yes. If you listen when a label is being used for identification purposes, it is most often used in a negative or derogatory way. Also, when you group all people together and add a label to them, you are pretty much saying that "They" are all alike. The Jews, the gays, the far right, the blacks, the Cubans etc. By using labels, you eliminate the chance of getting to know someone as an individual. On the other hand, when you take the time to get to know someone as an individual, you often gain a whole different perspective.

More importantly, using labels is the easiest way possible to create division among people or groups. The mission of One Planet United is to help eliminate division among people and I would say that a great place to start is to be aware how you use labels when referring to others. If you choose to look at others as "Those People" and don't take the time to get to know them personally, you are only helping perpetuate division in our society.

For peace to be possible in our world, we need to come to a higher place and the best way I can see to get there is to begin to use a whole new label when we identify others. It is called The Human Label. If we begin to identify others as fellow human beings and do away with all the labels that are currently creating division among us, we have a much greater chance of experiencing a world filled with peace and harmony.

You Already Belong

As part of something inside us, human beings inherently want to be identified with something. Whether it is a symbol or a cause, a group of many or just a few, we feel a sense of belonging if we attach ourselves with something.

What do you attach or identify yourself with? Do you have a bumper sticker on your car that signifies who you'll be voting for in November? Or what school your child may be an honor student at, attaching yourself to being a good parent? Do you have a Jesus fish logo attached to your bumper or an American flag as your front license plate? Does your favorite tee shirt or sweat shirt have the logo of the sports team you die for each week or does your prize golf shirt make a statement with the logo as to where you have played golf? How about the caps people wear? Doesn't it look odd if someone is wearing a cap with no logo or message on it? It's hard to find one that is blank. How about designer clothes? RL, DKNY, TOMMY, GUESS and many others. The various companies spend millions of dollars on designing a concept, look and symbol or logo that they hope you will attach yourself to. The next time you visit your local supermarket or town mall, see how many people you pass that have a name, symbol or logo attached to their clothing or car. It might surprise you how many there are.

No matter what, we as human beings want to attach ourselves to something because we want to belong. It is inborn in the human psyche. ONE PLANET UNITED asks you to think of belonging in a new way. In a much *bigger* way. Be a part of something that can't be cornered into a separate group. Begin to be a part of a raised consciousness which is, that everyone in the world belongs to the same group; the family of humanity. Begin to think in a much larger way. A way such that we begin to realize that *we are all one* and regardless of how we unconsciously find ways to be attached and belong, realize that we all "fit in" already. One man to another, one woman to another, one heart to another. Be assured you already belong, and you are already attached to the greatest group ever. The group we call the human race.

The Opposite of Equality

Feeling equal to others feels pretty good. For some, feeling superior to others feels even better. It's kind of an ingrained thing in lots of us that if we can feel a little superior to someone else, we often feel a deeper sense of self worth and security. If we live in a nicer neighborhood, drive a higher class of automobile or have graduated from a "status" college university, does it give us that little feeling that we are better than others? What about education and degrees? One person has barely made it through high school while others have Bachelor degrees and PhD's. Is this how we measure superiority amongst human beings?

What is at the core of this kind of thinking and relating to the world? What is the need in humans to attach themselves to a feeling of superiority over others? I bring this topic to light mainly because I continue to see many forms of this type of thinking which I believe are at the core of many of the ills in our society today.

Can you not see it in the way one particular religion claims that their religion is the only true path to God, thus portraying a feeling of superiority over people of other faith expressions? What about the liberal left vs. the conservative right? Do not both of these groups denounce the other as inferior in their belief system? I still see this regarding racial issues as well. When I hear someone refer to any minority as "those people," a sense of equality cannot exist.

So what is the opposite of equality? It is called supremacy. When most of us hear that word, we only relate it to a racial term for prejudice known as "white supremacy" that is currently embraced by such hate groups as the KKK and the Aryan Nation Movement. The way I see it, supremacy as a way of thinking and relating to others is alive and well in many other ideologies. The dictionary describes a supremacist as one who believes that a certain group is or should be superior.

Rather than point fingers at any particular groups, maybe its best if we just take our own personal inventory. Do I practice religious supremacy? It's likely if I claim to know the absolute truth and do not honor others who are on a different path. Do I practice political supremacy? There is a good chance if I make fun of and belittle those from the other party. How about patriotic supremacy? Do I feel that Americans are superior to people from other countries? Depending on my gender, do I harbor feelings of supremacy toward the opposite sex?

The list goes on and on that includes other areas such as financial status, sexual orientation, and even the company you work for. It is all a mode of thinking that has to be rooted out if we are ever going to live in a world where we honor and respect all people, even though they might be different from us in many ways.

The term "white supremacy" is one that we are all familiar with and the damage it has been responsible for in racial circles in our society. We must look for and become conscious of any and all feelings of supremacy that we might hold in our hearts toward others and do all that we can to eliminate them from our lives. If we do, then equality will reign and in equality there is the possibility for peace, brotherhood and good will toward all.

"Who Are The Real Heroes?"

The headline on a recent front page of South Florida's largest newspaper read: "Hometown Heroes." It was the lead story that had all of south Florida in celebration mode. Many fans of the Miami Heat, approximately 250,000 strong, had lined the streets for a parade to celebrate their team winning the NBA Championship for the first time in franchise history. Personally I have lost the interest I once had as a die-hard Knick fan growing up in New York, but I was one of those who stayed up well past midnight as the games were exciting and the outcome wasn't known until the last seconds ticked off the clock.

The headline of "Hometown Heroes" was somewhat disturbing to me though. If we want to headline heroes in our world, are these the guys we want to focus on? I bring this point to light based on my belief that we are teaching young people that the heroes of today are grossly overpaid sports stars, rappers with made up names and movie stars and music icons that make their way through each day with entourages and body guards.

Well, I have to say, these folks are not real heroes and it is up to us to teach our children thus. Stories of the real heroes of our day are often not found in print and if they are, you won't find them on the front pages. You can find them either toward the back of a daily newspaper or weekly magazine or not at all.

Hardly anyone will ever hear about most of today's real heroes because what they do normally does not make the headlines. For those that do, I applaud a few who use their celebrity to qualify as true heroes. Rock singer Bono has become an activist to expose and help heal world hunger. Another rocker, Jon Bon Jovi, has donated millions of dollars for outreach in the Philadelphia area, building playgrounds and purchasing clothing and school supplies for inner city youth. Angelina Jolie is using her celebrity today as an activist for healing in Darfur and Congo, where cruelty, violence, death and hunger are the order of the day.

I want to tell you about a real hero that only a few people know. They were able to meet her and hear her story at a recent One Planet United Community Celebration. Her name is Karen Bossert and she was honored on this particular night as One Planet United's First Annual "Humanitarian of the Year." Karen is a very anonymous lady who has devoted her life to caring for emotionally and physically challenged adults at a group home called Hatikvah House here in Coral Springs. Her day begins by waking at 5:30am to bathe, dress and feed five adults that do not have the ability to care for themselves. She then sees that "her guys" get to their day care, therapy and recreation throughout the day, finding small gaps of time to clean the house and prepare for the evenings duties and activities. For limited pay and long hours, Karen says her life is full by being of service to those in need. Her life is used to be eyes for those that can't see, a voice for those who can't speak, legs for those in wheelchairs, and ears for those who can't hear. To me, Karen is a real hero.

There are many heroes like Karen in towns and cities across the world, but their stories don't make the front page. Seems like tragedy, war, violence or glorified athletes and celebrities fill that spot.

Until we awaken our consciousness as a society as to who the real heroes in life are, we will still most often, be glorifying the wrong people. I challenge parents to seek out the real heroes in your own community and teach your children that these people are the people to honor and emulate. Sometimes they are hard to find, because often, the work they do does not appear in the headlines. When your children begin to know what defines a real hero, they too one day, might embrace the idea of becoming one themselves which can only make our world a better place.

We See the Heart Once More

One more time, the true hearts of everyday human beings shone as a bright light in a place of darkness. Not unlike other events that put aside human differences, I had the overwhelming experience of taking part in an event where love and care for a fellow human being pushed aside some of the things that can often separate us as human beings. This time, competition and profits.

I'm talking about being involved in a fundraiser event for a young man in his early thirties who had been recently diagnosed with germ cell cancer. He has already begun chemotherapy sessions and other healing modalities, but unfortunately is getting little help from health insurance and disability. The reason this event was special and different is that this fellow was a sales representative in a very competitive industry. His job on a day to day basis was to go out and sell his products and convince his retail customers that what he was selling was superior to all others in the market and that his service could not be matched. The real facts though are that he was also going up against many other sales reps selling similar products who all felt the same way he did. So day after day all of these men were out on the road doing what competitive sales rep do. Mainly doing whatever it takes to convince their customers to buy from them and not their competitors.

When it was learned that this man was diagnosed with cancer, a very strange but powerful thing came into being. One of the sales reps from a competitive company and a retail store manager came up with an idea to put together a way to try to raise some funds to help a man in need. They began to discuss it with all of the different sales reps who work in the Broward, Dade and Palm Beach county areas. They suggested that they might ban together and hold a fundraiser for this man and his family. They were aware of his plight as to how his bills were going to mount up and that he was going to be getting little outside help from any insurance agencies. Add to the fact that this man has a wife and two small children and was just starting on a dark journey of trying to recover from a potentially deadly disease. It was agreed to by seven or eight of these men that they would hold a golf tournament and invite anyone they knew from their industry as well as neighbors, families and friends. The tournament was officially named "You've Got a Friend."

What happened next was that as this tournament began to grow, the retail stores that were also competitors with one another began to come together to promote the tournament with the customers that visit their stores on a regular basis. Not only were all these different folks committing to play in the tournament, many of them were also volunteering to donate gifts and prizes that would be given as raffle prizes and auctioned off to raise additional funds.

After six weeks of hard work helping build this tournament into a successful event, the day arrived that all these people from a very competitive world were going to join their hearts together in unity to help a fellow human being in need. You could hardly think of another time or place that people who in the day to day world that all are looking out for themselves, their businesses and their profits, could come together and leave all that aside. This is where One Planet United understands that when human hearts touch and souls are united, the things of our world that we think are important become extremely insignificant. It shows us that when pain and vulnerability become present in our lives, the human heart can put aside differences, prejudice and even competition.

Once again, it was a time to see what we all saw on the tragic day of Sept 11th, or the day of the massacre at Columbine. For a time, we all forgot about our differences and prejudices and became united as one heart in humanity. We became what Neale Donald Walsch has called "Humanity's Team" where we only see all the people that we come in contact with as fellow brothers and sisters regardless of what they do, where they live, what color they are, etc. Let us once more use this example as a model to remind us that peace among all people is possible if we see first the heart and the soul of all human beings. We need not wait for tragedy to strike to put this way of living into practice. You can begin today.

Special note: At the end of the days play in this one day golf tournament, Mark Peterson and his family were presented with checks and cash that exceeded $30,000.

Forgiveness at the Highest Level

Once again, we can know that there are many lessons that can be learned in tragedy. Just recently an entire community of people was turned upside down and inside out at the hands of a gunmen whose inner pain and demons drove him to slaughter five innocent young girls while in the end, taking his own life as well.

I'm speaking of the Amish community in Pennsylvania that, three weeks ago, was visited by a mentally ill man whose only way to deal with his anguish was to execute innocent young children. Families and friends of the slain girls were shocked, bewildered and deeply saddened but something was very different about this tragedy. Missing from the Amish people were calls for revenge, protests in the streets, an outcry to the N.R.A. or the usual outrage that follows such a tragic event like this.

I know I am not alone when I first learned of the response from the Amish people. I was at first totally stunned and then I found myself in a state of awe of what happened next. This is what I heard and saw. The Amish people felt or displayed no anger toward the man who devastated their community. Their response the following day was to seek out the family of the deranged man and offer their hand in forgiveness. They met with the killer's family and said because of their faith, they hold no anger—only forgiveness.

Is anyone surprised at this response? It can lead you to feel one of two ways. You could figure that the Amish people are out of touch with reality and in a state of denial or you could see it as a group of people who truly understand forgiveness and do not return violence for violence. Is this possible? What would we do if it was our family and what would our reaction be?

This brings me to the thought of many of the discussions I have had with those who think that we should "get" anyone who "gets" us. These are the same people who most always believe that war is justifiable and that the death penalty is a good thing for society. After all, isn't it supposed to be an eye for an eye and a tooth for a tooth?

It seems the Amish people really live the message that was passed to us most notably by Jesus who said, "Love your enemies and do not take revenge on someone who wrongs you." He also said, "When someone strikes you on the cheek, do not retaliate. Turn the other cheek."

When I write this, it is only to show that there truly are people living on our planet that understand the true message of forgiveness. It's what I call forgiveness at the highest level. Maybe we can all learn to bring this into our own lives.

I wish I could honestly say that I personally would act the same way if it was my family but I don't know if I'm there yet. I can only hope that I am.

Let us learn from such a devastating event and let us offer up a prayer to the young girls and the families of these sweet innocent souls that departed this world all too soon.

In memoriam: *Naomi Rose Ebersol 7, Marian Fisher13, sisters Mary Liz Miller 8 and Lena Miller 7, and Anna Mae Stoltzfus 12.*

We Are the World

We are the world, we are the children. Happy twentieth anniversary to a song that hasn't been heard in a while. It's hard to believe but it was 1985 when "We are the World" hit the airwaves with an impact that inspired the planet. This song was said to have been written in twenty four hours by some pretty famous people from the music industry such as Quincy Jones, Michael Jackson, Lionel Ritchie, the late Ray Charles and a host of others. From what I remember, the project was called "U.S.A. for Africa" and was put together as a music album to be sold as a fundraiser with the proceeds being donated to Africa for relief from hunger and A.I.D.S.

I remember a feeling that seemed to be in the air at that time. There was a sense among millions of people of the importance of reaching out to our neighbors whether they lived across the street or on the opposite side of the globe. It had some of the same feeling that we all experienced on 9-11 or most recently with the tsunami disaster.

The vision of One Planet United continues to believe that it is possible to have this same sense of love, compassion and care for all of humanity each and every day. It was brought to my attention once again last week during a sold out concert I attended last week by the musician and composer, Yanni. He not only presents a powerful musical performance, he shares a humanitarian message as well. In the middle of the show, he took a break to introduce the musicians that perform with him. Their were approximately twenty five different musicians and they were literally from all over the world. Before he introduced them individually by name he introduced them as an entire group. This is what he said to the audience.

"Before you stand some of the finest musicians in the world today. What I want to share with you is that we are a very diverse group. We represent many different nations. We represent many different religions. We represent many different philosophies and we represent many different schools of thought." He paused for a couple of seconds and then proceeded to say, "But … we make beautiful music."

I have always admired Yanni's humanitarian messages that are always sprinkled in between songs as he performs, but this particular message was one that the whole world could benefit from hearing. The question is, "How can we make beautiful music with all people we share this planet with?" Or another, "How can we recreate the unifying sense that we are the world?" Here are a few suggestions that could set us in the right direction. Search out and let go of any and all prejudice you harbor in your heart. Lose any feeling of superiority you might feel you have over any individuals, groups or institutions. Each day, make it your mission to reach out to someone in need. And finally, pray to the God of your understanding that you be a person that is helping to unite the human family by your acts of love, compassion and kindness toward *ALL* people.

Celebrating Humanity

Does the title of today's column sound a bit strange? What do you mean celebrate humanity? Is this something new? When it comes to celebrations, the list we currently participate in is quite extensive. We celebrate birthdays, anniversaries, special days such as St. Patrick's Day and Valentines Day, and major religious holidays that include Christmas, Easter, Hanukkah and Ramadan. We celebrate the birth of the U.S.A on the 4th of July with fireworks displays that often take our breath away. Many cities around the country hold cultural and regional celebrations in honor of a particular ethnicity or lifestyle. In each celebration, there is one thing missing. Someone is usually left out. Not on purpose. It's just because the occasion doesn't fit.

Well, if you were fortunate to be present at The Coral Springs Center for the Arts a few weeks back, you were part of a very special celebration. One Planet United was host to over 800 people in its inaugural "Unity in our Community" celebration with the theme being: "Celebrating Humanity." 150 performers danced, sang songs, performed drama presentations and spoke from the podium all celebrating humanity and encouraging everyone present to put away the many walls of division that separate so many human beings. Included in the program was a special video presentation honoring Karen Bossert as the First Annual One Planet United "Humanitarian of the Year." Karen gives her life in service to humanity by caring for many mentally and physically challenged adults who reside at Hatikvah House, a group home in Coral Springs.

The purpose of this event was to bring awareness to the fact that celebrating humanity and the things that all people have in common is what can change our outlook on an every day basis. We tried to create an atmosphere where people knew at a deep level that "loving your neighbor" is something that we should strive to achieve on an everyday basis. Also brought to the attention of those in the audience by the keynote speaker, Dr. Paul Veliyathil, was the need to eliminate labels that we give to one another so we can see that at the core, we are all human beings. He pointed out that we often see ourselves and others as members of a particular religion, race, class or political view. Dr. Veliyathil said if we eliminate these kinds of labels that most often create division, we could then become a united people.

So after this special evening, I have to say I'm all about celebrating humanity on a daily basis. And if we all choose to celebrate humanity, this means everyone on the planet can participate. Of course, not everyone was born on the same day (birthdays), married on the same day (anniversaries), is Irish (St. Patrick's Day) or in a love relationship (Valentines Day). Some folks don't practice a particular religion or are not patriots or even Americans for that matter. But all people on the planet share one thing in common that we can all celebrate; that we are all human beings which is the one label that contains no division and where no one can be excluded.

In closing, it's my wish that the celebration of humanity becomes as common as all the other days and occasions that we have come to celebrate on a regular basis. Begin to know that if the collective consciousness of all people celebrated humanity, cherished humanity and embraced humanity, their could not be wars, violence, domestic and child abuse, racism, prejudice and all of the other social diseases that keep peace out of reach for us all. I guarantee you that if you begin to look at every person you come in contact with as a member of your own human family, you'll find cause for a very special celebration!

The Four-Way Test

Have you ever heard of the Four-Way test? I imagine for most folks the answer would be no unless you happen to be a member of the Rotary Club. The Four-Way test was brought to my attention a few weeks ago when I was invited by the Rotary to be their luncheon speaker. One of the members had heard about One Planet United through a friend so he called me and asked if I would speak about the mission and programs of OPU.

The regular luncheon announcements were made regarding information about fundraisers that the club was involved in as well as other important upcoming events. The last item on the agenda before I was introduced as the day's speaker was the affirmation of "The Four-Way Test." Everyone in the room stood and repeated the mantra that stands for the beliefs and values of all members of the Rotary Club, not only in this local chapter, but around the world. In unison, they repeated together, *"Of the things we think, say, or do, Is it the truth? Is it fair to all concerned? Will it build goodwill and better friendships? Will it be beneficial to all concerned?*

As I was introduced, I couldn't help but comment on the mantra I just heard all the members reciting. I said the Four Way Test could change the whole world if every person on the planet adopted the principles. I also said that the mission and vision of One Planet United could be found in this profound statement.

The major focus of One Planet United is to promote the equality of *all* people as well as uncover ways to eliminate or lessen prejudice, intolerance and division among people in all its forms. When I heard the Four-Way Test recited, I was excited and proud that OPU is helping to promote these same principles and that we have such a strong alignment with a great organization like Rotary. Every program we promote teaches fairness, equality and goodwill toward others.

OK, please bear with me for a minute while I dream a little bit about what could be. What I mean is—what would it be like if all racial differences related to the Four-Way Test? How would the scene in the United States change if all of our elected officials lived by this oath? How would gays be treated in our society? Would wars among nations exist? Would divorce among couples who were once deeply in love happen as regularly as it does? Would corporate executives be able to steal from their employees? Would road rage exist?

So you want to live in a world where people get along and care about one another? Where crime does not exist and vulnerable people are not taken advantage of? One where we all see each other as members of the same human family? A great way to begin would be for all of us to take The Four-Way Test and put the principles into practice on a daily basis. If we do, it is sure to rub off on many of those around us, in particular our children, who ultimately are the future of the world.

Note: The Four-Way Test was adopted by the Rotary in 1943 and has been translated into over one hundred languages.

Now You're Getting Personal

Mel Gibson says he was drunk, Michael Richards aka; Kramer, says he was angry and Tim Hardaway was just talking off the cuff. In recent weeks another insensitive outburst by a celebrity has made the national headlines. I'm talking about radio talk show personality Don Imus, who when he was referring to a mostly African-American girls basketball team from a major college university as "nappy headed hoes," he said it was all in the spirit of comedy. The list goes on in this past year that includes political conservative Anne Coulter and star of the #1 hit show Grey's Anatomy, Isaiah Washington. They were both exposed for their inappropriate and insensitive remarks about gays.

Today's column is not about picking on celebrities and trying to make them look like villains. It is to open a dialogue about understanding that prejudice seems to be a part of all us and to say that as we evolve as human beings, we need to use incidents such as these as opportunities to grow and change.

As I followed the media's coverage of this event involving Don Imus, I heard a comment from one of the members of the basketball team that I believe is the message we can take and learn from. The team was being interviewed on national TV and one of the girls said, "What hurts most is that he could use such a terrible slur toward me and he doesn't even know me." What a powerful statement this young woman put forth because it truly speaks of the underlying core of most prejudice, intolerance and bigotry that is alive today.

As part of trying to make amends and bring healing to this incedent, Imus agreed to meet with the team in person and offer his deeply felt apology to all of the girls. What ensued as part of this meeting is that he was given the opportunity to get to know them personally. By meeting them, they became real human beings and this is where it all changes.

A few weeks back these were just a bunch of nameless, faceless girls who happen to play basketball so to use a derogatory slur when referring to them was not to difficult to do. After meeting with these girls, he now had a human experience and connection with them. After this type of personal contact, what are the chances he could ever use a slur again when referring to this group of girls he has taken the time to get to know? He had just met a group of bright, friendly, energetic and well adjusted girls who now have names and faces.

Today's column is called "Now You're Getting Personal" which is my call for all of us to do just that. It is highly unlikely that racial, religious or sexual slurs could be used about someone you personally know. Does it seem possible that someone would use a derogatory term for someone who is gay if they had a close friend or relative that was gay? Could someone tell a joke about a Catholic priest being a child molester if their brother was a catholic priest? Could someone make an off the cuff remark about Jews if they had close personal friends who were Jewish?

Let us all move forward and continue to grow toward realizing that all human beings are to be honored and respected with the highest amount of dignity regardless of whether we know them personally or not.

CHAPTER 2

Religion

We're Getting There—(Part 1)

I recently read an article that I'm sure would get some folks upset, but from a One Planet United perspective, it gave me hope that we, as a people, are getting there. Where is there? "There" is a place of religious unity among all people of faith.

The article was a report on this years National Prayer Breakfast held this past February in Washington D.C. Among the 3,500 in attendance were some of the world's most powerful people, many whose lives have been positively affected by prayer and personal faith. This event has been held annually for more that 50 years and it was designed for the purpose of bringing world leaders together to come before God in prayer. This year's keynote speaker was rock legend Bono, whose address focused on the need to end poverty, AIDS and world hunger.

What struck me most in the article was the fact that King Abdullah of Jordan was also on the dais to address a mostly evangelical Christian audience. It was the first speech ever at the National Prayer breakfast by a Muslim head of state.

The fact that he was invited to speak shows that we are evolving as a people and that we are "getting there." His address was mainly focused on the need for religious unity and the end of extremism in all of its forms. In focusing on this issue, King Abdullah said;

"At this point in history, our service to God, our countries and our people's demands that we confront extremism in its myriad of forms. Extremism is a political movement, under religious cover. Its adherents want nothing more than to pit us against each other, denying all that we have in common. To overcome this common foe, we must explore the values that unite us, rather than exaggerating the misunderstandings that divide us."

President Bush's address to the audience this day also spoke to the need of unity among people of faith and how all people must come to a place of tolerance and understanding with those who might experience God and faith by a different expression. I find it interesting that many believe that President Bush would not preach "tolerance" or pluralism in any way for the fact that he calls himself an evangelical Christian. For many evangelicals, these unifying concepts are not embraced. It might surprise many as well that our president has made many statements about religious belief and understanding that don't always align with the traditional evangelical view. In November of 2003,

President Bush and English Prime Minister Tony Blair were holding a joint press conference in London. Near the end, one of the reporters said;

"Mr. President, when you talk about peace in the Middle East, you've often said that freedom is granted by the Almighty. Some people who share your beliefs don't believe that Muslims worship the same Almighty. I wonder about your views on that." President Bush' reply was, *"I do say that freedom is the Almighty's gift to every person. I also condition it by saying freedom is not America's gift to the world. It's much greater than that, of course. And I believe we worship the same God."*

I conclude by once again saying that I believe we are "getting there." I speak of unity in all ways, not just in Religion. I see the collective consciousness of the world changing for the better. You might think that's a little strange based on what is currently happening in the world with war, greed, violence, and the like. I choose to see the time we are currently going through as a period of pain that is necessary if we are to reach new realizations. "No Pain, No Gain" fits here just like it fits an athlete whose eyes are fixed on an Olympic medal. The mental and physical pain was what made victory possible.

We're Getting There—(Part 2)

A few weeks back, I wrote about my belief that there are many encouraging signs that much of the division, ignorance and fear embraced by many who consider themselves religious, to be loosing strength. Religion is often used as much as a tool to divide people as it is to unite them, but there are continuing signs that many in the religious culture of our society are reaching a higher consciousness.

My continued excitement as to how we are "getting there" comes from a recent article that appeared in USA Today. It was a report about a religiously diverse school district in Modesto, California that decided to take a risk and bring religion into the classroom. In an almost unheard of undertaking for a public school district, a world religions and religious liberty course became required for all 9th grade students. Parents had the option to remove their child, but none chose to.

The report went on to say that it was the belief of the 115 member committee of community members and educators that it was time to embrace the idea of studying the major religions of the world in the hope that a new understanding among students would be the result.

Some parents feared that their children could possibly be subject to altering their current beliefs and creating a deeper division, but the good news is that only positive results were evident. A new understanding was unfolding among students who most often kept to "their kind." Bringing religious beliefs out in the open increased student respect for religious liberty for two reasons. First, students emerged from the course more knowledgeable about world religions and were able to have a new understanding regarding those who embraced different faith practices. Second, students learned that major religions of the world mostly shared the same moral values. When the administrators asked one student why she enjoyed studying other religions she said, "All my life, I've been a Christian and that's really the only religion I know about. So when I take this class, I see there are other religions out there, and they kind of believe in the same things I do."

We still have a long way to go, but examples such as this bold move in Modesto are a sign that we are slowly "getting there." Many who hold a conservative view in their chosen faith are not likely to embrace progressive moves such as this example, but it is my belief that knowledge and understanding, which are being created by strategies such as this example in Modesto, are the keys to ending much of the fear and prejudice that often undermine the good that is in religion.

How awesome would it be if all children were taught from an early age that religious diversity will always be with us and that people who embrace a faith practice different than their own are to be embraced equally as beloved children of God.

So let's keep progressing forward in our pursuit of a broader and higher way of thinking. A narrow view, when it comes to religious practices and beliefs, has proven to perpetuate deep division among people of faith and worse, as we are currently witnessing, the pain, death and despair of war. It is time to open our hearts to accepting one another, respecting one another and ultimately loving one another. If I'm not mistaken, when it comes to all religions, isn't this the ultimate goal?

The Shift

I feel a shift happening in our society. It is a shift of religious thought and interpretation. I see this as something that is newly alive and evident and will be a very positive thing in general for all of society, particularly those who choose a religious or spiritual path.

What is this shift I am referring to? It is a movement in religion that is taking many to a higher consciousness. I am a big believer that we are all spiritual beings at our core who are having a human experience and I feel that this realization is coming to the forefront for more and more people of faith. We are truly waking up!

The shift I see is this. It is a shift away from a mode of thinking that is common today among many people of faith. They are beginning to challenge and question belief systems that have never been questioned before. Many of these beliefs were handed down from generation to generation. Some include that in God's eyes, we are unworthy and intrinsically bad, that all babies are born imperfect (original sin), that God is a vengeful God, that God is of the male gender, that God is out there or up there (the man upstairs) somewhere either up in a cloud or beyond space, and that God has favorites which means that when we die, certain people will be included in the kingdom while others will be "left behind."

I see more and more that this belief system which divides and separates people from God, each other and all of humanity, is fading away and a new consciousness is unfolding. A new consciousness—a shift—that believes that because we were created as divine children of God that we are worthy and that we are born pure and whole. This is being called today, by many modern day theologians, the concept of "original blessing." Continuing is a belief that is unfolding that God is unconditionally loving and that it is not in God's nature to be vengeful. Also, that God is inside all of us and not "out there" or "up there" somewhere. That all faiths are equal in the sight of God; and that "Us and Them" is shifting to "Us and We."

Some will say that this shift is bad for people of faith but many of today's leading theologians are seeing it more as liberation from a fear based theology. A theology that truly stifles love and unity among all people, mainly because as people relate to God, they will also relate to themselves and others.

The world has changed, the world is changing, and the world will continue to change. I see this happening and I believe we are slowly learning, when it comes to evolving in our religious thought, that this is not blasphemy or dangerous. It seems that the evolution of religious thought is a threat to many. Think where we would be as a society if we did not evolve in the areas of medicine, science, travel and communication. We might still be living in caves or believing that if we reach the end of the earth, we will fall off.

Up until just recently, the evolution of a higher consciousness in religious thought has been pretty much stifled. I believe the shift is beginning and that if we are to become a united planet and a united people, believing that God desires this for us all is a good place to start. At this special time of year that radiates with love, joy, hope and promise, let us all open our hearts to this higher shift in consciousness. It will be for the good of all humanity.

"Fact or Fiction?"

A little more than a week ago, a new film was released that has seemed to bring fear to many in certain religious circles. It's the movie adapted from the book written by Dan Brown called "The DaVinci Code." What is this fear that I am referring to? We'll I have my own feelings and beliefs as to what it's all about and as always, I write from my own perspective.

What the fear is about I believe is that many Christian pastors, priests and lay leaders are worried that the film will have some of their flock begin to doubt their faith and question certain beliefs that have been held for centuries. They seem to feel that if they don't warn their followers of the potential harm that the film can cause, that people are going to be swayed to believe that all or some of the story line is true, thus making believers question their faith. The end result could mean that many who once held unshakable beliefs regarding their Christian faith might not "buy in" anymore and ultimately back away altogether. Was Jesus married? Did he father a child? Has their been secrets buried by the hierarchy of one Christian denomination that if found out, could change many of their long held beliefs?

First off, I'm worried that if a movie that is based on a book that the author clearly states is fiction can undermine someone's foundational faith, I wonder if their faith was built on rock or sand. Second, isn't a good thing that people of faith "renew their minds" constantly by questioning what those "in the know" tell them? I constantly get in theological discussions with many people and one thing that makes me question that someone's faith is solid is if they back up what they believe over and over with the phrase, "Well, I was taught ..." My thought is that if your faith is grounded on what you were taught, rather than what you have investigated for yourself as to what YOU believe, it has to be a very shallow faith indeed.

I think the best thing The DaVinci Code will do in the religious community is begin to challenge people to question much of what they have been taught. It will wake many up who have just been grazing in their faith like cows or sheep. Blind obedience, which many people of faith follow, does not allow for growth and personal reflection and study and this film will encourage many to investigate what they truly believe for themselves.

I believe that the fact that Jesus challenged authority on a daily basis is what got him killed. If he just went along and did not question authority and age old teaching, his murder would never have happened. Jesus' teachings were routed in questioning those who were supposedly "in the know." Jesus confronted, questioned and probed time after time.

I guess the big question seems to be "So is the DaVinci Code really fact or is it fiction," and my answer would be, what difference does it make? Faith and belief can't come from a book or someone else's teaching or belief system. Jesus said the kingdom of God is within us all and the only way we can truly access this kingdom is not by watching a movie or staying away from it. We can only truly find this kingdom by going deep within our own souls. It is only there that we can find the true holy grail.

Put a Little Love in Your Heart

The title of today's column comes from a hit song recorded in 1969 by Jackie DeShannon. It was the same song that was used as the closing song for last weekend's second annual "Faith in Music" interfaith musical concert. It would be hard for some to believe it but here is what the scene looked like. After two plus hours of individual performances from ten different music choirs, 2 soloists, and a liturgical dance group, all 295 performers joined together on the stage to sing the closing song. Jews standing shoulder to shoulder with Muslims, Christians sharing the microphone with Hindus and Bahai's, all joined at the level of the human heart to express that they see one another as brothers and sisters of humanity and that religious differences really do not matter when one human heart is connected to another.

The "Faith in Music" interfaith concert is one of eight community building programs created by One Planet United that are designed to bring unity and understanding to all people. This particular program though is meant for the religious community specifically. It is meant to bring awareness to the fact that although people of varying faiths often shop for groceries in the same stores, cheer for their kids at the same ball fields, get their oil changed at the same garage and call on the same police and fire departments when needed, they pretty much avoid each other when it comes to hanging out in religious circles. They really never get the opportunity to learn more about one another or have any possibility of becoming friends. In the safety of their own religious community, most will stay close to their "gang" and never take the opportunity to mix with those from other faith communities.

That all changed on this particular night. It was a beautiful thing to see and experience. Those in attendance expressed that their hearts were opened, one religious community embracing another and that this was the first time they had an opportunity to see how other people expressed themselves in music and dialogue. One man said that he was going to take what he learned that night, which was a deep love for all people, and bring it out into the world every day. In a shared email the day after the concert a woman wrote, "What an amazing evening! The theatre was electric with beauty and love. I felt blessed to be there and I learned more about the "us" of all."

It's unfortunate that all people of faith do not get the chance to experience a spiritual community of love that goes beyond religious beliefs, doctrines and rituals. Some purposely stay away for what I see as a fear that their own religious world might be shaken by "religion mixing."

It has been said that words cannot express what the heart already knows for sure. The love that was expressed in this evening was at a deeper level—that being at the level where human hearts connect. It is at this point that the power of love goes deeper than words can express.

As the final song went on for over five minutes and all 1,300 people present joined in singing together, it was impossible not to experience a sense of the love of God at the deepest level. Although each and everyone's understanding of God might have been a little different, the love of God could not have been mistaken for anything other than just that. This night it was expressed in a united way, each person of faith sharing with another, that God is Love and Love is God. So, let's all put a little more love in our own hearts and see if we can spread this love to everyone we touch each and every day.

Division from Within

Once again, I was amazed at the deep division that is often seen among people who practice a particular religious faith. You would think that I would be talking about one particular world religion that holds a different view of God and the world over another. Or that of a particular denomination *within* a particular world religion that can't seem to agree on doctrines or certain beliefs thus creating a divided view of faith. Well, my story today is quite incredible and I might not have believed if I had not experienced it personally.

My wife and I were on a trip a few weeks back up in the Blue Ridge Mountains of North Carolina. We had the opportunity to spend a couple of days with some old friends who used to live here in South Florida, but who were now enjoying a very restful and enjoyable time of their lives in retirement, living in a small town thirty miles south of Asheville.

One of the things I love to do when away on a trip, whether it be in another state or another country, is to experience religious services that are happening there. I assumed that because our friends were very active in their local church as they had been in other churches all of their lives, that my wife and I would be invited to attend their church with them on the Sunday morning of our visit. They said they would rather just go out for a leisurely brunch and that they would be OK with skipping church because their congregation met two other times during the week. I asked my friend which church in town he went to and he told me the Baptist church. I had told him that I had seen a couple of Baptist churches in town and wondered which one he and his wife attended. He corrected me and told me that there were *four* Baptist churches in town. From what I recall, he said that one was called Baptist Southern Convention, another was Baptist Free Will, the third was called Baptist Reformed, and the last was Baptist Missionary. I was stunned when I heard this. Four different church congregations from the same denomination of one religion in a town with only 500 residents! He explained that they all held varying beliefs of the Christian faith and the Baptist denomination. I asked him if these churches ever joined together to share in worship, fellowship or community outreach and he said that does not happen.

Please know that I am not picking on the Baptist denomination of Christianity. For sure, there are other divided denominations within Christianity as well as in many other religions. I bring this story to light to point out how common it is and how this practice creates such a large barrier to a united planet among people in general but especially for those who follow a religious path.

The One Planet United column is always trying to expose the many ways that human beings divide themselves from one another. Of course you would think one of those ways would not be through religion. Unfortunately it's true. Isn't religion about loving your neighbor? Isn't it about prayer and asking the God of your understanding to root out hatred, differences, and barriers that keep us from loving our fellow man (or woman)?

Something is wrong with this mode of thinking and I say it's time we recognize this as extremely divisive and detrimental to unity among people. It is time we wake up! I don't believe we will ever unite all world religions as one and that probably is a good thing since human beings need different faith expressions to align with who they are, how they were raised and what they believe. But can't we at least bring together all denominations of a particular religion, especially different expressions of the same denomination, so we can experience unity, love and understanding with one another?

It is time. It is time to come to a higher place. Only good awaits us if we do. Only unity awaits us if we do. Only true love of our neighbor awaits us if we do.

A Different House of Worship

One Planet United is always on the lookout for the many ways we separate from each other in our society, and is continually looking for inspirational ideas to breakdown barriers. Whether that is from across a continent or across the street, we all need to become aware of the many ways we divide ourselves from others. We often think it is most prevalent when one country disagrees with another and the possibility or reality of war exists. The fact is most divisiveness takes place right in our own cities and towns in our day to day existence. We break off into our groups or gangs and often do not even notice.

The one that is my focus for today's column is our religious expression. On a weekly basis, families and individuals gather together with their chosen religious group to express their love for God and one another. But it most always is done with your chosen group that fits you best. We seek out religious and spiritual services weekly in our response and desire to worship God as we understand him. We attend Christian services in churches, Jewish services in temples, Muslim services in mosques and Bahai "Firesides" in people's homes. There are also many denominations within the same body of faith that meet each week.

These weekly expressions of faith are a good thing for most people. We learn to continue to focus on positive life giving principles, our children are taught the tenants of our faith and we participate in fellowship with our "like minded" friends. On the negative side of this human practice, this keeps us from ever really knowing people of other faiths, thus keeping us divided one from another when it comes to religion. We build walls by being dedicated to "our faith."

For a day or a short time, One Planet United has come up with an idea that can open our eyes to the many different expressions of faith that can help us all to become bridge builders. For one day, let's leave the familiarity and comfort of our own house of worship and visit one totally foreign to us. In the next month, make a commitment to visit another house of worship different from your own, and witness how other people express their love for God and their desire to grow spiritually. There you will see and meet an entirely different group of your neighbors and fellow human beings who for the most part are a lot like you. If you are Catholic, go to a Baptist Church. If you are Mormon, visit a Methodist Church., or maybe if you are Presbyterian, go to a synagogue or mosque to worship. If you are Jewish or Muslim, try a Lutheran or Unity Church. If you are Bahai, Hindu or Buddhist visit the house of worship that is the closest to your home, but is not of your same faith or denomination.

By joining in on this idea, you will help the mission of One Planet United to continue to grow. The mission that we are truly one people living on this one planet and at the core, we are not really so different from our neighbors. We can continue to grow in the knowledge that there is a big and mighty God who loves and cares *for us all* as well as come to know that although many do not share my same religious belief, they are seeking the same things in life that you are.

A Fundamental Problem in Religion—(Part 1)

Today's column is part one of a two part series that asks the question, "How can such a good thing like Religion turn out at times to be such a bad thing?" The answer is when it's followers use it to promote and live out their prejudice, hatred and bigotry toward people they don't like or don't understand. Isn't religion supposed to be a good thing that helps people get through tough times and become better human beings?

When do you know if Religion has gone from being a source of spiritual growth and inner strength, to a weapon used to separate and divide? In Part 1, One Planet United wants to address this issue from a Christian perspective. Personally, I embrace the Christian faith for my strength and inspiration, but I also have a love and respect for all people, no matter what faith they choose to follow. I must admit, I've wanted to address this topic for a while now, but wasn't quite sure how to approach it. At the risk of stirring up a little controversy, I feel compelled to share my feelings.

To be honest, at times I am quite embarrassed to let people know that I am a Christian because of the bad name that Christianity is often given. At the core of all this is Christian fundamentalism which is brought forth by some who speak a language that I do not endorse and hardly understand. To define Christian fundamentalism exactly is not that easy but as I have heard of things similar, you know it when you see it. From what you see and hear on Christian television and radio, to the bumper stickers that some people display, one would think that only "their group" is in favor with God. That only their group will be "saved." They have the belief that their way is the only true way and that all other people are lost. It has the same feel to me as a group of folks who use to wear white hoods claiming that there was only one true race, that being the white race.

Christian fundamentalist's claim that they are only following what the Bible tells them, but I must be reading a different bible than they are. Fundamentalists find scripture versus that they can use to fuel their prejudice and make themselves feel better than others in God's eyes. It is my belief, as well as that of many other Christians I know, that all people are equal in the eyes of God and that the Bible should not be used to threaten, scare or coerce people into embracing the Christian faith. I'm all for anyone who has strong beliefs and convictions in what they believe, but it all changes when others are not allowed the freedom to believe as they feel led to believe.

Fundamentalist's often find verses in the Bible that separate and divide while at the same time, many verses can be found that unite all people of faith and those whose God might not be Christian. Here is a few to look at. Luke 10:25 Jesus says: *to love the lord YOUR God.* Ephesians 4:4–5 Paul says: *there is one body and one spirit and that there is one God and Father of all people.* John 5:24 Jesus says: *you must believe in him, who sent me.* I presume he is talking about believing in God, more importantly than himself. Acts 10:34–35 Peter says: *God treats everyone on the same basis and those who fear him and do what is right are acceptable to him, no matter what race they belong to.*

These type of inclusive verses are scattered throughout the Bible, but the fundamentalist only uses the ones that are based in fear and division. I started today's column by asking; when can religion go from a good thing to a bad thing? I say when it is used to separate and make you feel superior or when you are going to tell someone that they must believe as you do or be "cast out" of God's camp. Could this be a form of bigotry and prejudice with a Jesus mask on?

Stay tuned for part two in my next column. I'll touch on some additional views of the destructive and divisive side of fundamentalist Religion as well as many views that can draw us together in unity.

A Fundamental Problem in Religion—(Part 2)

Today, One Planet United will continue to look at the harmful effects of fundamentalism in Religion as well as look at some of the inclusive ways that others choose to see God. You would think, from the emails I received after part 1 of this column, that there truly is only one way to God, and that a certain Christian group is truly redeemed and all others are lost. That is one of the main issues I am addressing with this topic. The thought that someone can know that there is a "true path" and that if your are not following it the way they believe, you are not in favor with God. Is it really possible to know what God thinks or who God truly is? It has been said that a candle to a moth is an overwhelming light, but it is sure a dim imitation of the sun.

This rigid and often self righteous and divisive way of thinking once again separates people into "us and them." The need for people to live in this "us and them" world often gives them the same feelings that other supremacy groups thrive on.

Is their such a thing as religious supremacy? I believe there is and I have seen it with my own eyes and heard it with my own ears. As a person who has been a follower of Jesus Christ for over 35 years, I have interacted with hundreds of Christians, and it is scary how some of them hold on to this belief that they are "saved" and others are lost. They get this information from four or five verses in the Bible and as I had pointed out last time, there are as many *inclusive* verses in scripture as there are *exclusive*. This is why it is impossible to get into arguments about the Bible, because two people can interpret things to mean two totally different things, depending on their belief systems and backgrounds.

Since last weeks column spoke mainly to the harmful effects of Religious fundamentalism, today will touch on more from the inclusive side of spiritual belief. I received a Christmas card from a couple a few years back and it touched me so deeply that I have since framed it and displayed it on a wall in my home. The picture has five little children from different nations of the world and they are all playing with a little bird. The message states, "God made so many different kinds of people. Why would he allow only one way to serve him?' It made me think of a scripture from the Old Testament that says, "The righteous of all Nations shall inherit God's Kingdom." If we could all embrace this belief, we could then come closer to becoming One Planet United.

Mother Theresa, a devout Christian and servant of God, never used language or a way of thinking to separate people and their beliefs. She was once asked if part of her ministry was to covert those that she reached out to and her reply was, "Of course I convert. I convert you to be a better Hindu or a better Muslim or a better Protestant. Once you have found God, it's up to you to decide how to worship him."

I often think that it takes a group of like minded people to form a belief system of any kind, whether it is a healthy or unhealthy one. Without a group of people to agree on something, you're left alone by yourself to decide what you feel and believe. Groups form belief systems as well as religions and denominations of all religions. Individually, you have to think for yourself, which often times is harder to do. Well, what happens if there are not enough people to form a belief system when it comes to worshipping God? I am reminded of a time a few years ago when my family and I were on a summer vacation in Colorado. We had rented a car and were traveling in some very desolate country. We came upon a town called Twin Lakes, which had one store, one gas station and one church. The population could not have been more than one hundred people and the next closest town had to be fifty miles away. I wanted to get a closer look at what denomination the church was and was deeply moved by the sign on the front. It read "We have one weekly service, Sundays at 10:30 a.m. We gather and worship God together." There was no mention of Religious affiliation or denomination. I realized with so few people, they had no choice but to worship together. They didn't have enough people to form groups and create separate houses of worship. I thought, if this was the way we could all worship, the very large problem of divisiveness in Religion would be eliminated.

We can only hope and keep on praying that those who see their path as the one true way, thus dividing themselves from all others, will wake up. I'm talking about waking up to a new consciousness and knowing that the righteous of all nations shall inherit God's kingdom.

When Religion Becomes Evil

I have just begun to read a book that was recommended by a friend and realized after only twenty-five pages that is one of those books that you find so powerful that you can't wait to turn to the next page. I've only read about ten books in my life that would fall into this category of "Wow" on every page. I've always been fascinated with Religion and its powerful force in the world as well as in individual people's lives. I have often said that if I was starting my life over again as a college student looking for a course of study, I would pick World Religions as my main course of study.

The book is called, "When Religion Becomes Evil" by Charles Kimball. Charles is a professor of religion and chair of the department of Religion at Wake Forest University. He is also an ordained Baptist minister, who has spent his life studying all the worlds' religions. I find it a little unusual, yet very encouraging, that an ordained Baptist minister would be able to view religious faiths other than his own, as worthy in Gods eyes.

The subtitle to the book is "Five Warning Signs." He is trying to bring to light the dangers that can be brought forth in Religion if certain things become extreme. His five warning signs of corruption in religion are: *absolute truth claims, blind obedience, establishing the ideal time, the end justifies the means and declaring holy war.*

Today, One Planet United wants to address the first warning sign, "Absolute Truth Claims." We have touched on this subject in the past but believe it is topic that continually needs to be brought out into the light. OPU believes that this way of thinking is the fuel that keeps certain religious people divided from one another, and keeps the "us vs.them" mentality going, which is a great form of harm in our world. Any kind of thinking such as this will for sure keep us divided from our neighbors and keep us feeling special and superior in some way, which is the danger that Charles Kimball is addressing.

A statistical study says that 6.2 billion people live on this planet. Broken down by religious faith, the largest group of followers falls into the category of Christians at 1.8 billion followed by Islam (Muslims) at 1.3 billion. It means that half of our population is following a different path or no path at all. I can only speak from my own experience as a Christian on some of the deep beliefs within this community which I believe to be extremely harmful. Not all, but some denominations of Christianity thrive on the belief that their way is the only true path (absolute truth) and that all others are lost and not in favor with God. If I had to take an educated guess, I would say that maybe 25% of the 1.8 billion Christians believe in this exclusive way of thinking. If we do the math, that would mean that about 5 ½ billion people living on our planet, according to some Christians, are following a false path. Can 5 ½ billion (550 thousand million) people be wrong?

By claiming absolute truth in any way, shape or form, someone then has to be inferior to you. We have seen in the past, in religion as well as other areas, the harm that this type of thinking and relating to others can do.

My wish going forward is that we grow closer to the belief that no one can or should proclaim that their faith is the only true path and that all others are false. One of the bumper stickers I continue to see says, "Pray for the U.S.A." Why not add to your New years resolution list to instead, "Pray for the whole world" and the unity of all religions.

We would then be one step closer to peace on earth and good will to all people. Wishing you a happy and blessed holiday season.

The Opposite of Love is Fear

Is there any story bigger in the world of religious news right now than that of the motion picture "The Passion" and its creator, Mel Gibson? It has created a buzz, some of that being excitement while some of it being controversy, but one thing is true. When it opened at the box office last week, many were turned away because of theatres being sold out. It is my feeling though that a very large percentage of those that are flocking to the theatres are mostly evangelical and conservative Christians, and not those that the movie seems to be more aimed at. Mainly people who don't take religion seriously or practice any spirituality in their daily lives. Those folks will most likely be lining up to see *Mooseport*, *Along Came Polly* or *50 First Dates*.

I have mentioned in the past that I am a follower of Jesus Christ and a true believer in the goodness of the Christian faith, but as it looks right now, I'm not sure if I will be seeing this film. I've already seen a number of interviews with those who have seen it as well as Mel Gibson's one on one interview with Diane Sawyer. What I'm taking away from these interviews is that the film was created as some will say, to show God's love for mankind through the suffering of Jesus, but I sense it has maybe even a larger agenda. That being, the theme of a lot of Christian materials, which is to create fear in people that if they don't believe, they are risking God's wrath. This is the part of the Christian faith that I have never believed and have never been able to comprehend. The fact that Mr. Gibson's main focus is on the last twelve hours of Jesus' life and the torture he had to endure while only bringing in brief flashbacks of his ministry is what has me puzzled. Gibson admits in his interview with Ms. Sawyer that the theme of the movie is taken out of context and that he stated in the interview, "I wanted it to be shocking, extreme and push people over the edge." It made me question what was at the core of his thinking? The fact that a large portion of the beatings and torture of Jesus are filmed in slow motion as well as frightening and eerie music a constant in the background seems to be enhancing the drama, but for what purpose? If the film was to be made as real and authentic as possible, why the Hollywood special effects? Could it be to manipulate the emotions of the viewer?

Yesterday, I joined a discussion with two evangelical Christians who were talking about the Diane Sawyer interview and how great this movie will be. I told them I have my problems with it. I told them that I feel an underlying theme in this movie uses fear and manipulation in getting people to pay attention to the gospel message and that my feelings were that this would not be the approach of Jesus. I said I believed that he would draw people near to him in an approach that didn't use gore, violence and manipulation. Even though they both said they agreed with me, one of them said quite seriously, "some people need the hell scared out of them."

The main focus of today's column is really not about this movie or Mel Gibson. It's mainly about my observance of the different ways Christians relate to a God of love and forgiveness. I often think if Jesus were trying to draw someone near to him, would he use the fear or manipulative approach? His love was surely extreme and his ministry certainly pushed those in power over the edge, but when he was attempting to touch the hearts and souls of people who were lost, afraid, or in need of forgiveness, didn't he used kindness, gentleness, compassion and love? Many Christians think that the fear based message is the one that should be used to draw people to God, but I've always asked, WWJD. "What would Jesus do?" Would he use fear or scare tactics to get people to follow him? I thought of this a few weeks back when I saw a bumper sticker on the back of a $60,000 Lexus that read: "If you are living like there is no God, you better be sure." Underneath the phrase, were flames coming up simulating a picture of Hell. This is a way many Christians believe the message should be presented. Sort of like, you better believe this way or else. I thought, if Jesus was alive today and he owned a car, (I'm guessing it would not be a Lexus) would he have this statement on his bumper sticker to try to draw people to him? My thought is that his bumper sticker would probably read something very simple like, "Love One Another."

It also brought back in my memory when my daughter had been attending a youth group years ago when she was of middle school age. She returned home with these little cards that she was urged to give out to her friends to bring them to a belief in Jesus. On one side of the card, all it said was "Know Jesus"? And when you flipped the card over, it referred three Bible verses as a reference as to how to know Jesus. The first thing I noticed was that all three scripture verses were from the apostle Paul and the epistles, not quotes from Jesus and the gospels. The second thing that I noticed was that all 3 versus were fear based messages, such as "The wages of sin is death", and "All have sinned and fallen short of the glory of God" First off, you would think that if the front of the card referred to how best to know Jesus, you would see quotes from Jesus, not Paul. Secondly, is the way of fear the way Jesus used to draw people to him? Is this the way we should be teaching children to bring Jesus' message to those who have not met him yet?

From my experience of sharing with hundreds of people of faith over the years, I have found that there are two distinctively different ways that Christians see God. One is a fear based theology and the other is a theology based in love.

The thinking of "Fear God" stays true with many Christians throughout their lives, while many others come to believe that the true definition of that phrase, which many scholars agree, means to "Be in awe of God." Although I seem somewhat in the minority, it is my belief that Jesus endorses the latter.

Uniting People of All Faiths

Upcoming on Thursday May 6th, The City of Coral Springs will be observing the 16th Annual National Day of Prayer. What began as a Christian outpouring to God for peace in our world has become an event shared by people of all faiths in our community. Although the main theme is always to lift up our nation and our world and ask God to show us the way to peace with all mankind, the beauty of NDP in Coral Springs is that we invite *all* who believe in God, no matter what name we call God. The idea is to join together as one body of faith to pray for peace and to leave our theological differences aside for a day.

For most houses of worship in our community, this opportunity is a way to learn about others practice of faith and to be able to see that there are truly many similarities and beliefs that we all share. Unfortunately though, there are still a very few who do not participate because they believe it is hypocrisy to join together with people who worship a God by a different name than they do. Being a member of the interfaith committee has given me a close up view as to the few that do not participate. Last year I volunteered to pay a personal visit to the few pastors who said they would not participate, to discuss the possibility that they would reconsider. I soon realized that my efforts to discuss the importance and benefits of interfaith relations were being vehemently rejected. One priest stated that they don't participate in political events. Another pastor told me that they do not participate in events where false Gods are being worshipped. Sadly, with this way of thinking, they missed a truly inspiring event that was a celebration of God's hand upon all religious faiths and beliefs. They could *not* prescribe to an ancient saying that many live by, including many Christians, that states "God has many names but only one spirit, that there are many paths but only one truth and that there are many thoughts but only one mind."

One Planet United has always believed that a major force that often separates human beings is Religion and the different ways we all perceive it in our individual lives. It has always been foreign to me as to how something that can be so good for us, (the practice of Religious faith), can be such a breeding ground for prejudice, hatred, and feelings of superiority. The question I always ask is; If God has made so many different kinds of people, why would he allow only one way to serve him?

A favorite poem of mine written by James Dillet Freeman reads:

"There are many ways to pray, as there are many ways to God.
The way of the bird is not the way of the fish.
The way of the babe is not the way of the man.
The way of the beginner is not the way of the master.
Yet there is no atom of creation that does not have access to God.
Each soul finds its way to God at the level of its own experience."

If you want to experience the many different paths that our community has found to God, as well as celebrate your own, come join us on the front steps of City Hall, Thursday May 6th at 7:00 pm. A child representing each body of faith will offer up his or her prayer for the healing of not only our Nation, but our whole planet. You will be joining Christians, Jews, Muslims, Bahai's, Jehovah's Witness's, Mormons, Hindus, Native American Indians, Buddhist's and others, as we all pray for peace. In addition, their will be special musical presentations in honor of our love for God and our yearning for unity and healing.

Come be a part of this truly unifying evening and see that the city you call home, Coral Springs, is a small part of a large World, praying for healing and peace.

On Being a Witness

If you are a Christian, you most likely have heard the importance of the great commission. This is where one is told in the scriptures to go out into the world and make disciples for Christ. You are urged to tell others of the "good news" of the gospel story.

Over the years I have come to notice that there is a vast amount of ways that Christians follow this idea.

The first and what seems to be the most popular is telling people with words. Many Christians use words to tell others about their faith, and depending on where their faith is found, those words can vary in great degree. I have written about this in the past, but it continues to amaze me that two people could be sharing what looks like the same basic message, and use words that are as opposite as night and day.

I'm talking about how some share the message of their faith in a language that denotes fear while others use a language that is based in love. The slogans we see on bumper stickers, tee shirts and church entrance signs tell a lot of the story. I drove by a church one day and on the sign out front, it read "If you love God the most, you'll love others best." A while later, I drove by another church and the sign read, "Read the Bible everyday. It will scare the hell out of you." I would say that although these two different types of beliefs would claim that they are speaking of the same God, it would make many wonder.

This is why words often times are not the best way to share our faith with others. Words can often times mean different things to different people. Depending on how you came to your faith will most often dictate the way you share your faith story with others. In the Christian faith alone, there are over 250 documented denominations that all have their own slant on what they believe and how best to tell others about your faith. It can come from a place of gentleness and compassion or it can come in the form of a spiritual assault from the ivory tower of self righteousness as well as many interpretations in between. Depending on your life experience and the spiritual path that God is directing you on, words can take on different meanings.

One Planet United suggests that if we truly want to share our message of faith with others and respond to the great commission, let's put our words on the back burner and use our actions to tell the story. I have always been a big believer in the familiar slogan, "Actions speaks louder than words." The people I admire most that are living a life of faith say very few words. Their faith is mostly expressed in how they live their life and how they serve those in need. The best way *all* people can witness, Christians as well as those of all other faiths, is to try to live by the profound words of Saint Francis of Assisi who said:

"Preach the gospel all the time. If necessary, use words."

Finally, if you are looking to share the good news of your faith, try putting forth the action of your faith and follow the direction of a man who once said, *"I'd rather see a sermon than hear one any day."*

One Planet United offers up the following suggestions:

Support a charity of your choice with financial help, volunteer at one of the non-profit organizations in your area, read to the elderly, mentor a child, visit the sick in hospitals and nursing homes, spend time with those who are lonely, reach out to a neighbor, feed the homeless or just look for ways to help others that are less fortunate than you are. You will then be living out the great commission in its truest form.

A Different Kind of Bible Study

As I continue to embrace interfaith groups, programs and events, I find myself continually engaged in one on one conversations with people from many different faith and religious beliefs. It truly shows me that if we are to have our planet become united, there is a stronger need now more than ever to gain a deeper understanding of other religious beliefs so we can come to understand that there is a common theme that runs through them all. That being love, kindness, compassion and respect for all people. Unfortunately, there are some who don't want to think that there are possibly other paths to God. These are people who practice a faith of exclusivity, which is one of the big issues that perpetuate the inability to see *all* people as brothers and sisters.

With all the dialogue I have with members of many different faiths, what I find most troubling are the conversations I have with some members of my own faith community. I'm talking about when a person who calls themselves a Christian uses chosen verses in the Bible to tell others that they are on the wrong path and that they will not be "saved" unless they submit to the path that they are on. A person like this will use the same few "exclusive" verses from scripture to back up the fact that they know who will be saved and who will not.

I titled today's column "A Different Kind of Bible Study" where the object is to find out if there are scriptures and verses that are inclusive and give all people, Christians as well as people of other faiths, the same access to God both here and now as well as in the life to come. There are many places in scripture that speak of an inclusive God. Let's examine some of them.

The Gospel of John 5:24 states (Jesus speaking) "I am telling you the truth: those who hear my words and *believe in him who sent me* have eternal life" Jesus is saying to believe in God, not in himself. People of many different faiths other than Christianity claim to believe in God. This verse seems to include all people who believe in God. In the Gospel of Luke 10:25 it says; A teacher of the law came up to and tried to trap Jesus. "Teacher," he asked "what must I do to receive eternal life?" Jesus answered him, "What do the scriptures say? How do you interpret them?" The man answered, "Love the lord your God with all your heart, with all your soul, with all your strength and with all your mind; and love your neighbor as you love yourself." Jesus replied, "You are right. Do this and you will live." I see two distinct meanings of inclusiveness in this story. First, Jesus is saying to love the lord YOUR God. Second, I know many people of other faiths who follow this scripture to the best of their ability. Jesus is saying that it is the way you live your life and how you treat others that is the important matter, not what religion you practice. Acts 10: 34 (Peter speaking) "I now realize that it is true that God treats everyone on the same basis. Those who fear (respect) him and do what is right are acceptable to him, no matter what race they belong to." Finally let's look at 1 John 4:16 which says "God is love, and those who abide in love abide in God, and God abides in them." Sounds like God will abide in anyone of any faith as long as love is present.

As a follower of Jesus, I've never been one to use the bible as a divisive tool and I only bring these few verses to light to show that there are many verses in scripture that can be interpreted as exclusive and there are many that can be used to be inclusive. I believe that the Bible should be used in a personal way so one can gain wisdom and strength as they journey through life and seek to deepen their faith. It shouldn't be used as a divisive tool. I've mentioned it before, but the best way anyone can preach the gospel is by the way they live their life and not by taking a Bible verse that suits their belief system and then using it to let others know who is saved and who will be "left behind." I suggest we leave that decision up to God.

Note: "A Different Kind of Bible Study" is a study of the Gospels from an "inclusive" perspective. If you would like a copy, email me at jack@opunited.org I will forward it to you.

Religion and Police Work

I hesitate to write back to back columns on the subject of religion, but I continue to be so startled by some of the things I hear some of today's most noted religious leaders say that I feel it necessary to share some of my thoughts and feelings. I'm mainly talking once again about what I hear conservative Christians saying and believing. It's hard sometimes to speak out against what I see as extremely negative for as I have mentioned many times, my own personal faith is that of Christianity. From what I'm hearing of late though, I think I am going to go the route of a very close friend of mine who says he no longer calls himself a Christian. If someone asks, he refers to himself only as a disciple of Jesus.

The thing that upsets me most is not only *what* comments I hear, but *who* is making them. Tune in Christian radio or nightly FOX news and you will hear some of the most bizarre things coming from the mouths of some of the most influential leaders of the Christian faith today. First of all, it seems like they are always in a moral or political battle or war with a certain group or they're trying to "take back America for Christ." When I look at scripture and see what Jesus' agenda was, the only people he was at war with was the righteous religious leaders of his day. When he came upon sinners, outcasts and people who were morally challenged, he would gently encourage them to seek a better way. The way I see it, Jesus was extremely gentle and forgiving with the weak. On the other hand his attitude toward those who were the moral police was not what I would call gentle. In the gospels he refers to them as vipers, white wash sepulchers and hypocrites.

Here are a few examples of the dialogue I have heard in the past few weeks coming from the mouths of some of today's most powerful and influential Christian leaders. On this particular radio show, the host and a guest were having a discussion about the need to build up the numbers of total Christians in the world. In the middle of their dialogue, the host came out with a statement that made my jaw drop. He said "there is approximately 1.5 billion confessed Christians in the world today, which is almost twice as much as the next closest competitor." When you refer to other religions as "The Competition" and you have a lot of devoted followers that follow your leading, it certainly sets up a whole movement of people who see their faith as Us vs. Them, which is extremely divisive and harmful. This same host, who happens to be a pastor as well, was broadcasting his radio show on another day talking with a guest on how he felt that public schools were a breeding ground for immoral behavior and inferior curriculum. His next statement was "You will have to answer to God if you send your child to public school." I found his statement to be an embarrassment to the Christian faith and I also found it interesting that he is the founder of a very upscale private Christian school in Fort Lauderdale.

Another world renowned religious leader, whose father is the most recognized evangelist the world has ever known, was on FOX news a few weeks back and was asked "Did God send the Tsunami that killed over 200,000 people?" He said that it wasn't God but Satan who sent the Tsunami. He was then asked, "Well doesn't God have more power than Satan and couldn't he have stopped it?" His reply was that God gave Satan certain powers in certain situations and that he doesn't control everything. This incredible Q&A went on for almost 10 minutes with this evangelist trying to make sense out of this tragedy giving answers where there truly isn't any. Finally his last statement was "Well, what it really comes down to is that this whole catastrophic event is really a mystery and no one really knows why this happened." I was wondering why that wasn't his first response at the beginning of the interview.

Finally, the leader of a very large Christian organization from Colorado that has millions of loyal followers was asked a question regarding gay marriage and shouldn't he be practicing tolerance. His response was that "We don't embrace tolerance. If we did we would be approving of behaviors that are against biblical principles." This same man's son has just published his latest book titled "Be Intolerant." He claims that there is nothing wrong with righteous intolerance. When I read the gospels, I find that the people that upset Jesus the most had this same attitude.

In the long run, I don't see this type of rhetoric and type of theology drawing others closer to a life of faith. I see at as extremely divisive and damaging. If you desire to bring people closer to Jesus, I urge you to become a servant and be a model of his love and compassion toward *all* people. If you do, then others will have an opportunity to see what a true disciple really looks like. That of being a servant, not a policeman.

"Is *ALL* Life Truly Sacred?"

To say my heart is broken regarding the whole life and death situation of Terri Schiavo is an understatement. Many people watched and witnessed the death of a woman who was truly the only family member that had no voice in her situation. To watch the ongoing destruction of her family members from both sides was almost as horrible as watching her die. Unfortunately, even after Terri's death, it doesn't look like much healing will be forthcoming any time soon for the immediate family.

As tragic as this event was, there was something that left me puzzled and greatly disturbed. I'm talking about the protesters that stood in front of Terri's hospice causing a major disturbance night after night to an already troubling situation. From the beginning, this was a situation that should have been a very private matter for only Terri and her immediate family members. I felt very disturbed that the people who were claiming that *all* life is sacred and wielding protest signs with statements like read "Murder is a sin" used this sad situation to push their ideology.

What is more unsettling for me is that these are often the same people who are willing to also fight the abortion issue because to them, "All Life is Sacred." The problem is, if this is their true belief, they still have a lot of work to do. I want to ask them to look deeper into their belief system and be true to the statement that all life as sacred. Unfortunately, with most of these same folks, if you come to know their true feeling about the sanctity of life, there seems to be certain occasions that taking a life is perfectly acceptable.

Is it possible to stand vigil protesting in front of the place where a girl's life is about to end because of judge's decision to remove a feeding tube that is keeping her alive while on another night be sleeping comfortably in your bed at home as a prison inmate on death row awaits a lethal injection by an order from the same judge? Or is it possible to march and protest at a Right to Life rally or have a vanity license plate that says "Protect the Unborn" while at the same time display a bumper sticker that asks God to "Bless our Troops" whose job description is to kill the enemy?

My question is; is all life truly sacred or does it depend on the situation? If this view comes from a Christian perspective where it most often does and we asked WWJD (What would Jesus do?), would he find it acceptable to kill anyone in any war or apply a lethal injection to any human being on death row?

I feel that if a person believes that all life is sacred, than it can't be OK that a person is killed or put to death in certain situations. Maybe when we say "Well, they got what was coming to them" we should re-examine what the word pro-life really means. How can war and capital punishment be perfectly acceptable while abortion and the removal of a feeding tube be totally indefensible? Life is life and ending a life is ending a life. I want to encourage those who are Pro-life to be truly Pro-life.

My plea as I close is this. If you truly believe that *all* life is sacred and are willing to spend long and arduous hours marching in protest, please let your protests and marches include the front gate of any prisons that carry out the death penalty as well as the front steps of the White House whose current leaders at this time seem to believe that only certain life is sacred.

*Inter-*National Day of Prayer

A few weeks back we once again shared in a very special day called the National Day of Prayer. For the past six years I have had the honor of serving on the committee that puts this program together for the City of Coral Springs and it was my feeling that this year's program was the most heartfelt and special yet. For people who don't live in Coral Springs and are able to participate in this event in other places, they might find the way we choose to present the program somewhat different than the norm. For most cities and towns that celebrate this great day, the participants are most often times from Christian denominations only. I don't think it is done in this way because of any prejudice or bias. I believe it is because mostly Christian groups are the ones that promote it and talk it up.

Well, this is particularly why I feel that the way it is presented in Coral Springs makes the event that much more special and meaningful. Because our community is so diverse in cultural and religious beliefs, it is only fitting that our committee sends out invitations to every religious group that congregates in our city. Therefore, we have a multitude of faiths represented and we get to experience a whole different kind of celebration. This year, we sent out over forty invitations in which twenty six sent an RSVP that they would participate. Those in attendance included people representing many different religious faiths including Buddhism, Hinduism, Judaism, Christianity, Bahai, Islam, and a representative of the Native American Indians. What made this event even more powerful was that within all of the different religious faiths were people from many different nationalities that were representing their faith. It certainly had the "One Planet United" feel and flavor that I believe is important for all of us to be a part of.

So you might ask, "What's up with the title of your column, Inter-National Day of Prayer? I thought this was the National Day of Prayer." Well, it's not a misprint. It is where I hope to see this great event grow to in years to come. My fellow committee members hear me each year say that my hope is that we will one day see this event become a global event and be called the International Day of Prayer. As of now, when we call it National, it means it is only celebrated as a regional prayer event. I want us to think higher and one day be able to celebrate in prayer with the whole world.

Once again, One Planet United is about all things global and universal. It is my belief that much of the turmoil we experience in our world is because we continue to see ourselves as separate from people from other countries. If we think regionally or just in terms of the United States, we might be one that embraces the saying that we see on many tee shirts and bumper stickers that says "Pray for the U.S.A." I'm a believer that we must think higher when we pray and "Pray for the Whole World." I actually had a few people come up to me and say they felt that some of the prayers being lifted up in this year's program were somewhat selfish and self-centered. I do recall some praying specifically for God to bless our troops, our President and our Congress. Shouldn't we go to a higher place and pray for the leaders of *all* nations as well as soldiers from both sides? What about when we put ribbons on our cars and offer up prayers asking God to bless our troops and bring them home safe? Are we also praying for the innocent men, women and children in Iraq as well that want peace as we do? And what about praying for our enemies? In the Christian tradition, it is a directive from Jesus. It is also promoted in many other faith traditions as well.

So if you are a person of faith and an advocate of the power of prayer, I challenge you to expand your scope to include all people on our planet when you pray. Ask God to bless all nations, not just the U.S.A. Ask God to touch and heal all people in the Iraq situation, not just American soldiers. Ask God to bless all world political leaders, not just President Bush. And pray mostly for our enemies. Come to a higher place in knowing that God is not on "our side" but on the side of *all* of his children.

Love Can Overcome Fear

Is there a new phobia on the horizon? From many recent newspaper articles I've read, websites that I see popping up as well as many offensive or sarcastic emails that come my way, I would have to say yes. According to a recent editorial in the USA Today, they agree as well. It is called "Islamophobia." The editorial says that mutual misunderstanding is the fuel that propels the twin phenomena of anti-Americanism and Islamophobia. If you ask me if I feel there is such a thing as Islamophobia, I would have to say yes as well. Because of my involvement with One Planet United and many interfaith events that I am a part of, I get the opportunity to dialogue with many people and learn what they think about issues such as this. I'll leave anti-americanism for another column. Today, I want to focus on this new fear that seems to be alive and growing.

A friend of mine and I were having a lively debate about this issue this past week. He sent me a few emails with statistics of the Muslim community and how they feel about the current situation in the world. He said that the problem is that the views of extreme Muslims represent 10–15% of a population that is estimated at close to 1.2 billion people worldwide. He figured that this means that over 120 million people sympathize or embrace the views of so called extremists. He also said that recent polls in London indicate that 6% of all Muslims felt that the recent bombings were justified. If you take the total number of Muslims in the world to be 1.2 billion, his figures said that approximately 72 million fully supported the London bombings.

If his math is correct, I choose to look at in another way. I said to my friend that if 72 million Muslims agree that the bombings were justified, that means that over 1.1 billion Muslims *do not agree* they were justified. I also asked him how many of the 72 million would actually strap a bomb on their body or fly a jetliner into a skyscraper to express their beliefs? Please don't misunderstand me. I'm not making light of the destruction that has and is taking place. It is known that only a few people who follow this path can do untold damage.

What I'm saying is that if we stay in fear, we will only let hatred and anger grow in our hearts. Personally, I have what some would think is a good reason to be angry at terrorists. A friend of mine who raised his family in the same neighborhood as I did was on the 90th floor of tower two in the World Trade Center talking with his wife on the phone when the second plane hit fifteen floors below him. He was never found. Sadly, he left four beautiful children behind as well as a very devoted wife.

What's seems to be the main fuel for Islamophobia is that many people look at Muslims as the enemy, when in fact it is not Muslims or the religion of Islam. It is radical extremists that use terror and violence as their tools to deal with their hatred and anger. The hysteria that is "Islamophobia" only perpetuates more fear.

I'm suggesting that we need to change our mindset and our hearts if there is a chance of healing. We have to find out why we are so afraid as well as try to uncover what the thinking is of those who want to destroy us. By remaining in a mode of fear and suspicion, we can't be effective in trying to be part of the solution. We will only continue to be part of the problem. We will continue to believe that the way to deal with violence is to fight back with violence. We need to look not with fear but with love. We then might be able to see where this hatred comes from.

Let's come to realize that most human beings want the same things in life such as a loving family and happy and healthy children. We need to keep things in perspective and not help perpetuate fear and anger toward a community of mostly loving people who like 99.9 % of the planet, condemn religious extremism and want to live in peace.

Voices in Unity

What do you get when you cross five world religions, ten musical choirs, three-hundred performers and an audience of one thousand people? You get religious unity, understanding and respect. Thus was the outcome at the 3rd annual "Faith in Music" concert recently presented by One Planet United. With singers and performers from many faiths and walks of life, once again the stage was set for people who normally do not mix in religious circles to come together and celebrate their faith through the vehicle of music. In today's world where religious division seems to be the norm, this particular evening showed that people of different faiths can unite and get along.

A Faith in Music concert is designed where each choir or group has a ten to twelve minute time allotment to perform for the rest of the choirs and the general audience. They are asked to bring their "best stuff" which they always do. These are choirs and performers that sing together all year in their weekly services, so the talent is always exceptional.

The most unifying part of the concert came forth at the close of the show. When it was time for the finale, all 300 performers were asked to join one another back up on the stage in a sign of unity. Here we saw standing shoulder to shoulder, those who embrace Christianity, Judaism, Hinduism, Islam and The Baha'i faith. They encouraged the audience to join them which resulted in the whole theatre singing as one. This year's email bag from some attendees included expressions such as:

"What a superb event last night!!! I quickly found myself rockin' in my seat and giving standing ovations."
"My family and I had such a wonderful time listening to the incredible talent displayed on that stage. Wow!"
"It was a truly inspiring evening. You all should be very proud."
"Thank you for preparing and serving another FABULOUS FEAST OF FUN AND FAITH!!!!!!!"
"It was so inspirational … I could hardly remain in my seat."
"My husband was very impressed with the show, and he doesn't impress easily."

Let's imagine for a moment if every city and every town brought those of different faith expressions together for an annual music concert. Could it be possible that the divide that is evident in much of religion today could be turned in a direction of unity and understanding? The mission of One Planet

United is to try to inspire others to take a leadership role in building bridges in our culture and to provide tools to do so.

Want to put on a Faith in Music concert in your community? OPU provides a template to show you how. No experience, education or training is needed. Only a small group of people devoted to help build bridges among people of faith. Visit the One Planet United website at www.opunited.org, click on "Programs" and then click on "Faith in Music" Concerts. Their you will find a template to follow that will provide a "step by step" outline on how to bring a Faith in Music concert to life in your community. All templates can be downloaded from our website and are free of charge. Best of luck and please be sure to send me an invitation.

Right, Wrong and Unity

A few weeks ago, I had the fortunate experience of attending a special inter-faith service that was held at The Unity Church in Fort Lauderdale. It was an extremely inspirational event in many ways that included music selections that made my heart soar, a tribute to the tragic events of 9-11 that reminded me of the importance of forgiveness and the main message that was quite unusual from a typical Sunday morning service.

The morning message was given in three separate 10 minute short sermons by the senior minister, as well as two invited guests. One was a rabbi from a nearby synagogue and the other was the executive director of an Islamic orga-nization whose mission is to promote peace with people from other faiths as well as to speak out against terrorism. I was deeply moved as this man read pas-sages from the Holy Scriptures of the Koran that spoke directly of the impor-tance of loving your neighbor as well as the condemnation of taking another person's life.

I was particularly moved by the rabbi's message which was that of trying to point out that no religion has the corner on absolute truth and that it is those who speak of knowing they hold absolute truth that do the most damage in our world. He pointed out that at the core of all indifference, intolerance and ter-rorism lies the belief that "We are right, and you are wrong." One group claims to have the truth therefore perpetuating a belief that all other beliefs are void of the truth and ultimately wrong. He said it was his belief that each religion holds a portion of the truth and that if we accept this, we can learn from each other and grow closer to our fellow brothers and sisters of all faiths.

The strongest point that he was making was the need to understand that we can have a unified world if we leave behind the feeling that we have to be right, thus making someone else wrong. He wanted us all to implant into our hearts a special saying that he said has been with him ever since he could remember. It is this:

"There is right, there is wrong, and there is unity."

When he said this phrase, it stuck with me throughout the service and for a long time after. I thought of the power that these ten simple words contain and saw the possibilities of healing of all kinds if we could all live these words in all that we do.

I thought about the destruction that affects millions in our world because of the need to be right. In marriages, in relationships with siblings and parents, co-workers as well as religious and political ideologies. I began to think if we weren't so obsessed with being right and having the other be wrong there would be so much more of a chance that we would know peace not only in our own personal lives, but with all people on our planet.

Maybe you have heard the simple question, "Would you rather be right or happy?" Somewhere, we as human beings have built into our personalities, a form of programming to fight to be right and have the other be wrong.

What are the possibilities of healing and unity if we could all focus on the Rabbi's message and not on who is right and who is wrong? I believe they are endless. His message is that if we can leave the need to be right while we make the other wrong alone, we can come to a true place of unity in many places in our lives. This simple philosophy has the power to heal all disagreement and fighting whether it is with our spouse, a sibling that we haven't spoke to in ten years, or with someone whose religious, spiritual or political ideology differs from our own.

We need to reach a new height in our thinking and consciousness about those we share this life with if we want to live in a world of peace and harmony. I truly believe that the rabbi's message holds the key. Why not adopt this philosophy in your own life and see if your personal life as well as your view of the world around you doesn't change for the better. Remember, there is right, there is wrong and there is unity!

A Thanksgiving Invitation

A community of faith will be joining together next Tuesday night and you are personally invited to attend. It is the Thanksgiving Interfaith Unity Service which is celebrated each year at this time by a collection of different faiths and congregations so easily found in our great city of Coral Springs.

I bring this service to the forefront in today's column to help gain additional exposure for one of our cities great unifying events. It seems that many folks that I talk to have never heard of this special event so I wanted to make sure to help get the word out. My wife and I attended our first Thanksgiving Interfaith service in 1995 and we have attended every year since. It is a special gathering of a very diverse group of people of faith all sharing in a common bond with one another; that being thankful hearts and open spirits.

This year's service really couldn't be coming at a better time for our community. It has been quite a devastating blow to many this past month because of an unwelcome visitor named hurricane Wilma. She wrecked havoc on many. Some folks had their homes and cars badly damaged while some had their landscaping pruned significantly more than normal. It seems though that we all suffered from an upheaval in our emotional and spiritual lives. Everyday routines and our mostly comfortable lives were turned upside down. I don't know about you, but I was made to realize that I live by a daily routine and it does not feel good at all when it is interrupted.

This special Interfaith Service will be held this year at First Church United Methodist Church. Each year the service rotates between different houses of worship with different clergy presenting a Thanksgiving message of unity. In addition, special music is presented by a choir made up of members from many different congregations that, for this night, become one voice.

This is a night that you will not want to miss. I encourage you to come and join hearts with many of your neighbors in Coral Springs to pray, to sing, to reflect on the difficult times we have all just been through and to give thanks as a community for all the many blessings that we do have.

Finally, I do know some people who are sometimes uncomfortable attending services that include faith beliefs other than their own. Why not look at it like this: If God is love, as *all* religions claim, I can personally guarantee from my past experience at this event, God will be there, so there is nothing to fear.

Bigotry and Religion

C'mon, what do you mean bigotry and Religion? Religion is a good thing. It is about love and kindness, compassion and loving one another. Religion is something good for all people, right? Bigotry, on the other hand, is the total opposite. It is a deadly social disease. So of course, you've got things a little mixed up. Religion and bigotry are total opposites. They can't possibly mix, can they?

Let's first look at a few definitions. It's probably better to look at the definition of what the word bigot means first. The dictionary defines it like this; Bigot—"One who is strongly partial to one's own group, religion, race or politics and is intolerant of those who differ." Bigotry is defined as; "The attitude, state of mind, or behavior characteristic of a bigot."

My inspiration for today's column comes as the result of reading a recent article in my local newspaper about a national assembly that took place gathering the largest branch of American Judaism for an annual conference in Houston. Rabbi Eric Yoffie, President of The Liberal Union for Reform Judaism, was the keynote speaker. He was addressing the dangers of bigotry in religion, and said it is found most evidently in the beliefs and practices of the "religious right." He said he continually hears the charge from the religious right that in order to be in favor with God, you must "attend my church, accept my God and study my sacred text." He asked the question, "What could be more bigoted than to claim that you have a monopoly on God?"

After finishing the article, I concluded that I could not disagree with anything the rabbi said. It is my personal belief that there is more bigotry and intolerance in religious beliefs and actions than there is in racial, political or sexual orientation issues combined. I believe it is a silent disease that keeps those with bigoted attitudes in religion unavailable to practice the true tenants of their faith.

If deep in your heart, you feel superior to another because of the path you feel inspired to follow, it is my belief you are not practicing the essence of your religion. If deep in your heart, you feel that your particular path is the only true path and that your group has a monopoly on God, I believe you are not following the essence of your religion. If deep in your heart, you somehow believe that you know for sure that all who do not follow your path are "lost," I believe you are not following the essence of your religion.

About a year ago, I wrote a column that challenged people to look deep into their own hearts and see if there was any prejudice, intolerance or bigotry in their own religious thought and in the ways they looked at others who experienced

God differently. I took a risk and shared my own personal feelings as a Christian and received a few emails stating that, considering my personal views, I should not be calling myself a Christian. I said it was my belief that whether you were wearing a white hood and claiming that your race was the superior one, or you were claiming religious superiority through the beliefs of your own spiritual path, that there really was no difference at the core. Bigotry is bigotry, no matter what the subject.

The core phrase in the mission statement of One Planet United is this; **One Planet United seeks to bring unity and understanding to *all* people**. With an attitude of bigotry, this is not possible.

In conclusion, I urge everyone to first review once again, the definition of bigotry and then hold the looking glass (mirror) up to your own heart to see if any bigotry lives there. If so, pray to the God of your own understanding to root it out. You will then know a new freedom and a new happiness. You'll see all people in a new and beautiful way as never before and you'll be a part of a consciousness that will unite us all.

Honoring the Divine in Us All

Last week marked the 5th annual Interfaith Service sponsored by Unity Church of Fort Lauderdale which was created to bring all people of faith together in remembrance of the tragic day of September 11th. It was a privilege and honor to be one of five-hundred plus attendees who joined hands and hearts praying that religious unity will continue to grow in our world.

The music was extremely uplifting and the morning message was shared by a Christian pastor, a Jewish Rabbi and a leader from the Muslim community. They each spoke of the need for all of us to continue to grow in consciousness that differences in religion are inevitable but that division does not have to be. Their words of compassion, love and understanding for one another touched all who were present and showed that religious unity is not only possible but absolutely necessary if a peaceful world is to exist.

In a Harris Poll taken a few years after 9-11, it was found that 69% of adult Americans believe religious differences are the biggest hurdle to achieving global peace. I'm not sure I would agree that this idea of differences is the problem, but rather the division that results from the differences. All three speakers shared some of the differences of each of their Religions but boldly stated that we can all learn to love one another, be unified as a people, and move forward in peace in spite of any differences.

I've always wondered why some people believe that if we are different in any way that this means we must be divided as well. The fear that keeps many people from embracing people of other races, nationalities, sexual orientations and the like has to be based on the belief that if we are different than this means we must be divided. This is a manner of thinking that we must rise above.

In a traditional Sanskrit greeting that has been practiced for centuries, people greet one another with a bow that means "The divine in me honors the divine in you." It has nothing to do with how you practice religion, what side of town you live on or who you voted for in the last election. It has to do with a deeper perspective. That being, that when I look at you, I see a person or a human being. This view eliminates any division because when we see only the person, divisions cannot exist.

In another poll taken a few years ago, 90% of the respondents said that they believe there is a heaven. This must mean then that they believe we have a soul as well. Let us then ask: What religion is a soul? Does the soul have a race? Does the soul have a gender? Does the soul have a political belief? Is a soul a particular nationality? It is my belief that when we see first the soul of another, we will then see the divine in them, and thus the absence of all division.

It is my hope and prayer that we as a society continue to evolve away from division and closer to the place where when we see another, our only thought will be, "The divine in me honors the divine in you."

A New Religious World

It's definitely not something that many religious people will be happy about but there continues to be a shift in the consciousness of more and more people that religion is being born anew. The term most often used is religious pluralism and it seems to be growing without any conscious effort on anyone's part. It is growing because we as a people are growing in our view of religious thought and practice.

Just recently famous protectors of their faith have come out and said it is time to lay aside religious differences and come and embrace one another. There is a recent call by many to love and honor those that happen to practice a different faith.

Evangelical Christian Billy Graham, now in his twilight years, has backed off from his belief that the only way to see God in the afterlife was through submission to Jesus. He said in a recent Time magazine article that he does not claim to know how God thinks anymore and that he will leave God in charge when it comes to who will make it to Heaven.

Nation of Islam leader Louis Farrakhan, also nearing the end of his life, speaks a whole new language when it comes to his past exclusivity claims of his faith. He is calling for Christians, Muslims and Jews to come together and to work for peace. Farrakhan spoke recently and said that the world is at war because people of different faiths are divided. He went on to say, "If Jesus and Muhammad were standing together today, they would embrace each other. How come we, the people of God, cannot embrace each other in the love of God and the love of the prophets we praise?"

In a recent study conducted by Diane Eck, author of "A New Religious America," she says that in the last 35 years we have become the most religiously diverse nation in the world. Ms. Eck, professor at Harvard University and director of the Pluralism Project, found that there are now millions of Muslims, Buddhists and Hindus living in America where only 50 years ago there were historically Christians, Jews and those that called themselves "secular." Back then if you mentioned the term "Religious diversity," you were speaking of Catholics and Protestants.

According to a 2002 poll taken by U.S. News and World Report which was designed to measure the acceptance of Religious pluralism, the following statistics were found. Only 17% of religious people believed that their religion was the only true religion and 78% of those polled said that they believed that all religions had elements of truth.

Catholic priest and expert on Islam, Reverend Phillipus Tule, has recently begun the practice of joining his young seminarian students with Muslim students for prayer and scripture reading. The students look for the value that comes from both the Bible and the Qur'an. Calling for a spirituality that unites people of different religions, Tule urges people to ignore traditional thinking that regards one's religion as the only true faith.

As I stated in the beginning, an evolutionary shift of this kind will leave some unhappy and uncomfortable that this is taking place. All change initially brings fear and discomfort but in the long run, we usually look back and see that the change was for the better. I believe that unity and understanding among people must begin with Religion and from what I can see, this type of shift has us headed in the right direction.

You Must Become as Little Children

A few weeks back I was fortunate to be a part of a very special event. It was the annual celebration of the National Day of Prayer held on the front steps of City Hall in Coral Springs. People from all faiths and houses of worship came together on this special night to pray for peace in our world and strength to reach out to one another in unity. This is a different kind of celebration from many other interfaith gatherings that I have attended in the past. What makes this event unique is that the people who are asked to share a prayer are all children from the ages of approximately 8 to 16. They come from all the different churches, synagogues and congregations in the community, but they are all united on this evening to pray for peace in our world.

I found myself in awe of some of the prayers that were shared by some of these children. They were offering up praise and thanksgiving to the God of their understanding as well as asking for guidance and direction for our city, state, country and world leaders. The innocence of their prayers as well as their ability to often see what are the important things we should all be praying for was a beautiful thing to witness.

The truth that children often speak and the hearts from where their words come, are something to behold. We as adults can learn quite a lesson if we tune into the prayers of children and heed their words. They usually pray in very simple words and often touch the places in our hearts where we should pay attention the most. The following unedited prayer is one of those examples that was written by a young fourth grade girl who seemed to know exactly where the chances for peace are the greatest:

"Dear Father God, I pray for World peace and that everyone will forgive each other more often. I hope that all the wars will stop and everyone will be OK. Please let all the people know that it's OK for not liking each other. Just try to be nice to them. Also, please show that people need to be more respectful to one another. People should try to be the best role model they can be for the little children. Please help us to respect other people's beliefs and religions. And help us to be truthful and faithful to ours. Amen."

This little girl spoke of all those things that are the answers to unity amongst *all* people. Things like acceptance, respect and tolerance of others, forgiveness, the need for children to have good adult role models and the end of wars. Could there be a better blueprint for peace?

On this special night the words that Jesus spoke over 2,000 years ago were still ringing true when he said, "You must become as little children if you want to experience the kingdom." The words and wisdom of these little children gave us all a little closer look at what the kingdom can look like here on earth.

CHAPTER 3

Politics
And
Patriotism

My Vote Stops Here

A man from Hollywood was quoted last week in the local Fort Lauderdale paper saying, "From now on, when two political candidates run negative ads against each other, I'm going to take their word for it. I won't vote for either one." He along with many others that I have talked to feel the same way and it's not just independent voters. It's moderate Democrats and Republicans as well. From what I can tell, only hard line Republicans and Democrats see a good purpose for the negative ad campaign strategy that has taken over our political world. It seems to help fuel their hatred for the other side.

How has it come to this? "This year in general, there are a lot of negative ads," said John Geer, a Vanderbilt University political science professor and author of *"In Defense of Negativity: Attach Ads in Presidential Campaigns.* "The reason for so many attacks this year is, the stakes are so high and neither party has a lot to run on."

Inevitably one side will win, but what does today's political strategy really accomplish? From the perspective of One Planet United, a more divided people and a more divided nation. If all of those running for office used only the strategy of declaring their goals if they should be elected, it would be more like a good competitive sports event where at the end, congratulations are offered to both sides. Unfortunately, the current campaign strategy of our public servants is driving a deeper wedge than ever between all people. For me, I've chosen to write an open letter to those running for office with the hope that they might begin to wake up and choose a different strategy.

"Sorry Charlie and Jim and Ron and Clay. I had no choice but to sit this one out. It got to the point where I reached my tolerance level and found it necessary to "Just say no." To what you might ask? I said no to going to the voting booth during last week's mid term election. I reached the point where I felt there was only one way I could have my voice heard in protest of all of your "negative" ad campaigns and dirty politics. It seems this year, you just went too far and I have a feeling that I am not alone in the action I took in choosing to pass. I tried to hear what issues you were running on and what you were proposing to do to improve the lives of all of us here in Florida. Well, I heard nothing of the sort. What I heard on TV and read in your ads was each of you bashing the other. All of you chose to demonize your opponents and constantly lob attacks against them as to how dishonest, lazy, or bad they were. You spent your time and tens of millions of dollars to point out what your opponent had failed to do and how I would be making a big mistake if I

voted for "the other guy." So it saddens me to say to you that unfortunately for this year, my vote stops here." Signed—Had enough

One Planet United will continue to speak out against any kind of division that pits one group against another and this issue is right up there at the top of the charts. If the current campaign strategy of today continues to grow, it is my guess that voter turn out will continue to shrink and one day only the hard-liners will be showing up. It's time to evolve to a new level of consciousness in all areas of life, but particularly in modern day politics. "To you Charlie, Jim, Ron, Clay and all future candidates—I hope you'll come to realize that your current strategy to attract voters is very destructive and helps to perpetuate division among people everywhere. In the future, I ask that you use a more professional and grown up approach. Just run your campaign solely on the issues and you can be guaranteed that many of us will return to the booth to cast our votes."

God Bless

I can't help but notice that with the renewed passion for patriotism and the displaying of the American Flag, the phrase "God Bless America" and "God Bless The U.S.A." are everywhere. It used to be the only time I remember hearing them was at the conclusion of the sitting President's State of the Union address. The President would close with the words "and God Bless America." At that moment, the audience would erupt in applause and the viewers on television would feel a sense of power and pride that God is truly behind the U.S.A.

Today, you can't pull up to a stoplight without seeing a bumper sticker that says "God Bless America" or walk into a supermarket without seeing a tee shirt or three printed with "God Bless the U.S.A." on them. One of the most powerful songs that is getting lots of airtime during these turbulent times is a song by country singer Lee Greenwood titled "God Bless the U.S.A."

OPU challenges us to take a little deeper look and ask ourselves when we use these phrases, "is our God to small?" In this vast universe we live in, the U.S.A. is just a very small part, so we are asking God to bless us Americans. Do we believe that God will really look after us, separate from the rest of the world?

I love being an American and I wouldn't want to live in any other part of the world, but I get more and more uneasy when I see or hear the phrase "God Bless America". How would we feel if President Bush ended his next speech with, "and God Bless the Universe" or if we saw a tee shirt that said "God Bless the Planet?"

Does standing behind the phrases "God Bless America" and "God Bless the U.S.A." promote the seeming arrogance some non Americans say we have? Is this part of why some say other countries hate us? Do these phrases cause division with us and the rest of the world? Even though these could be looked at as just a few innocent words, the impact they can have on our unconscious and our thinking is that it is us (Americans) and them (all non Americans), but the reality is, we are all human beings and equal in God's sight.

I'm a true believer that we should love our heritage, but we must always be conscious that we are a *world community*. If you are a praying person, OPU asks you the next time you see the phrase "God Bless America" or "God Bless the U.S.A." that you remember to add the rest of the world in your petitions for God's blessings.

"Politicians United?"

Somehow, I thought it would last, but I guess I was a bit naive. I'm remembering back to the Friday that followed Sept11, and I was once again glued to my television set watching the memorial service from the National Cathedral in Washington, D.C. One by one and two by two, political leaders who wished to have a place to pour out their grief and pain filed into the sanctuary. There was a strange thing though that was noticeably different. As the TV News cameras focused in on those attending, walking in together as well as sitting together were Democrat and Republican politicians from many areas of the United States. When it came to an event such as this, all of a sudden the term bi-partisan was brought forth and it seemed as if all in Washington, no matter what political party, bonded closely together in thoughts, prayers and feelings. TV news interviewers could not get anyone to mouth a partisan word and their unified responses signified that we are *all one people*.

Sadly, it hasn't taken long to have fallen right back into partisan land when any politician speaks or when right wing or left wing media views are aired. The war in Iraq was a perfect excuse to spout off partisan criticism and make the other party wrong. Also, the upcoming primaries for the 2004 Presidency are now upon us and the slandering has already begun.

What is it, that brings us to that place of oneness or in political language, Bi—Partisanship? Does it have to take a national tragedy that befell our country on 9/11 for these folks in high political places to abandon all of their prejudice against the "other party"? From what I can see, less than two years later, it is if it has all been forgotten. The feeling of being one, of being united, and of being of one single mind, heart and spirit, somehow has gotten lost once more.

One Planet United realizes it is good to have two or more viewpoints to protect people who might feel differently from one another. At the core though, we must always know in our heart of hearts that we are bound by the fact that we are all human beings desiring mostly the same things in life. OPU reminds these folks in Washington and in political circles worldwide, that their opinions and feelings are extremely small issues in the grand scheme of things. Let's remember that we are all in this together. Caring for and respecting each other, even though we might have different views from one another, should be of the highest priority.

We're All in This Together

Have you noticed lately that more and more cars and trucks seem to have an American flag attached either flying in the air or pasted on a sticker? It seems to me that almost every other vehicle has one affixed. I really think it is a good thing if the reason there are so many is for the sole purpose of supporting our troops at war in Iraq but somehow, I am uneasy with what could be another reason so many want to display the flag. It has to do with the words that are often along side these flags that say, "United We Stand."

When these three words are displayed, is this not the kind of thinking that could be detrimental to possibly achieving peace in the world? The main question would be, are we aware when we display this phrase that once again we are setting up an (Us vs. Them) way of thinking? In the phrase "United We Stand" I take the word "We" to mean, we (Americans). Well, if it is WE (Americans) standing united, who or what are we united against?

One Planet United believes that there is only one thing that should unite people as one and that is our humanity. The fact that we are all of the same race, the human race, and sharing this planet together should be what unites us. A flag should not be something that unites people, be it Americans or anyone else. If a flag unites us, it means that we separate ourselves from all those who are not from our own country.

There was a song written about 15 years ago by Julie Gold called "From a Distance." It was made famous a short while later when it was recorded by Bette Midler. It makes references that from a distance the world has no borders. There are no lines dividing cities, states and countries. We as human beings, created these boundaries and dividing lines. I know for certain reasons this could be looked at as helpful, but it has done a lot of damage also. It sets up a belief with many that somehow we are different than those from other places in the world, but the truth is, we are not. We are all human beings with hearts, souls and feelings. We may have different skin color or talk a different language, but at the core, we are all the same.

One Planet United is hoping that we can elevate our thinking to a higher consciousness going forward. To create healing of differences between countries and nations, it must begin with our thinking, one person at a time. Let's do away with the phrase "United We Stand" and replace it with, "United, *The Whole World Can* Stand." If we expand our thinking and begin to know that we are all in this together, true peace in our world will be that much closer.

When Patriotism Goes Too Far

Is it truly love of your country or a secret hatred or resentment toward non-Americans? From what I can see, there is a lot of both going on right now. I would like to start out today's column with a challenge to all those folks that are "Standing United," "Standing Tall," and whose "Colors Don't Run." and that is to have them ask themselves if their feelings are based in a love for their country and not bitterness and resentment toward "those bastards over there." I'm talking about all people from other countries that are not allied with the United States at the present time.

I often get the sense that there is a large part of our society that deep in their heart of hearts, hold a deep hatred and resentment toward non-Americans and that this hatred only continues to fuel the differences that divide us. I hear it in everyday conversations. I see it and hear it on radio and television news talk shows, and I go by automobiles every day with bumper stickers that validate my feelings. Last week, I pulled up beside a truck that was proudly displaying the most popular bumper sticker of the day which is the phrase "United We Stand" with the American Flag, and on the other side of the vehicles bumper was a very plain sticker that said, "Piss On France." It truly saddened me to know that this is what is in some people's hearts.

While many are not happy with the fact that certain countries are not our allies in fighting terrorism, what can this hatred be about? It is a continuation of the terrible spiritual disease of hatred of people from other countries that affects many in our society. When it crosses over this border, it can no longer be seen as patriotism, which is a healthy thing. It then becomes nationalism, which is very harmful to our world. Certain forms of nationalism are based in extremism and anything that stirs in this category is detrimental to peace and harmony amongst human beings.

Extremism is present in many areas of our culture such as religion, race, politics etc. Where does this type of thinking come from and how do some of us take what can be something good and turn it into something that is unhealthy and often dangerous. Since today's column is on the topic of "Love of Country," I will offer up a few thoughts that seem to me to be a breeding ground for this type of thinking.

Most of us when we were children were taught to love our country and place our hand over our heart when we said the pledge of allegiance. This is no different than when many of us were taught many of the religious traditions of our family's faith. We just said what they told us to say and eventually without giving much thought to what we were saying, over time these mantras became our beliefs as adults. How would we feel about others if our pledge of allegiance contained the phrase, "One Planet, Under God," instead of "One Nation, under God?" Where would our feelings for others be if we were taught to sing a song called the "International Anthem" that glorifies a world flag rather than the "National Anthem" that cherishes a star spangled banner?

A friend of mine sent me an email last week with an alternative version of "God Bless America" called, "God Bless the World We Love." If we were raised with this version, it's possible we would value *all* people as our brothers and sisters. Sung to the same music as God Bless America, it goes like this:

God bless the world we love,
Stranger and friend,
Go before us, restore us,
With the hope that despair cannot end.
Ev'ry people, ev'ry nation,
Mighty ocean, Heaven's dome,
God bless the world we love,
Our only home.
God bless the world we love,
Our only home.

This is once again a call from One Planet United that we need to first be aware if bitterness and resentment might be infecting our hearts and do whatever it takes to root it out. True peace in our world can only come when hatred and indifference are no more. We each need to search our own hearts and pray that the God we worship will clean out any hatred we hold for others. The founder of the Baha'i faith, Baha'u'llah, put it the best when he said, "Blessed and happy is he that ariseth to promote the best interests of the peoples and kindreds of the earth ... It is not for him to pride himself who loveth his own country, but rather for him who loveth the whole world." Let us all heed these powerful words.

"Please Don't Go There"

As the situation seems to worsen in Iraq and Afghanistan on a day to day basis, we all stand somewhat helpless to do anything to stop what is going on. We wait for the next piece of tragic news of more deaths and further destruction and wonder if further terrorist acts are headed our way. It is a very strange feeling for most adults alive today. There have been wars in the past of terrible proportion, but somehow this is at a different level. There is the daily threat of terrorism right here in our homeland as well as a degree of savagery in the way some of our country's people are being killed. It has become a time that we all are uneasy and our children are living in a time that somehow is impossible to relate to them what the real cause for all the unrest is about. Some will say it is America's arrogance that makes other's angry at us while others believe that it is just religious extremism gone amok.

Whatever the cause, we have to be careful to not let the events that have overshadowed us in the recent past form our attitudes of how we relate to those in the countries where most of the damage is being done. It really came to mind the other day when I was driving in my car and tuned in a popular radio talk show where the host was saying that he had had enough with all "those people" over there. He was extremely angry and said that he had reached a point that we all must realize that from now on it has to be either "Us or Them." He was adamant that it is time to realize if we don't get "them," they will get "us." He said that it is time that we go in with our largest artillery and just wipe out all towns and cities where we have any reason to believe that people who oppose us are hold up. It was kind of scary to listen to this kind of hatred being spoken about on a syndicated radio talk show.

As I listened to this radio talk show host spread his anger over the airwaves it made me think that this kind of thinking is exactly the kind of thinking that terrorists subscribe to. When he was referring to "them" and then referring to "us" it made me realize that if we choose to think like this, we will be harboring hatred toward an entire country of people when in reality, it is a minute percentage of extremists who are causing the damage.

The title of today's column is "Please Don't Go There." What I'm speaking of is the belief that if there are bad or evil people amongst a group of people, that they are *all* bad or evil. This is at the core of most prejudice and what is the fuel for the deep hatred that many people hold in their hearts. People often carry great hatred and resentment toward whole groups of people.

Let's ask ourselves a few questions. Are *all* catholic priests to be hated because a *few* have abused children in despicable ways? Are *all* CEO's of large companies now to be labeled crooked and dishonest because a *few* let their greed over power them at the expense of their dedicated employees. Should we consider *all* Police Officers as thugs because a *few* have turned an arrest into an assault of a helpless prisoner? Finally, should we consider *all* people from Iraq, Iran, and Afghanistan as evil because a few have chosen to use violence against those they oppose?

We have to be careful not to consider that because individuals choose to act a certain way that the whole of the group that they are a part of is to be labeled the same. If our children are growing up in households where they are hearing *all* Jews or *all* Blacks or *all* Gays or *all* foreigners or *all* people who are overweight or *all* anything are bad, evil or inferior, we are imprinting in them a hatred that is often dangerous and very detrimental to peace in our world.

The mission of One Planet United is to continue to expose many of the harmful ways of thinking that lead to division and prejudice. When it becomes "Us and Them" we set ourselves up to be blind to the goodness that is inside most people that we share the planet with. We must let go of any thinking that puts others in a category just because they live in a certain part of the world, have a different skin color than us or are different from us in any way. Until we know what's in an individual's heart, let's make sure we don't size them up as one of "Them." You never know, they just might be one of "Us." A human being, that is.

Left, Right and Center

Now that the Republican National Convention has come to a close, it's time for all Americans to sift through the information that both parties have passed along, and begin to decide who they will vote for on November 2nd. It is time for all people to figure out which candidate they feel will take us to a place of peace and well being. While each person is busy trying to figure out who has the answers to the ills of our society, I'll just continue to believe personally that neither candidate will have much of an effect. Let's look at the surface and then go to the core.

One of the reasons is that many of us remain a people divided even in our own country by subscribing to a particular party to stand behind. You would think it is the same as standing behind your favorite baseball team in a pennant race as the season is winding down. That type of partisanship doesn't really divide human beings on human issues and when it is all over, the scoreboard let's us know who the winner is. In political races, it goes much deeper. There is often what seems to be a deep hatred rather than a sense of "may the best team win." When you side with the right or the left in a "fan"atical way, it seems to me you have lost touch with the fact that "your man" will have little effect on the most important things that all people yearn for.

The negative comments from both parties that are being thrown at each other continue to perpetuate as we get closer to Election Day. Each party will take something out of context that can be construed as truth and use it to undermine their opponent. And what about those people who are on one side or the other but are not the candidates themselves. If they could only hear themselves. From the conservative right, Jerry Falwell says God is pro-war, so vote for Bush. As well, conservative Pat Robertson says that he really believes he is hearing from the Lord that George Bush will win in a blowout. From the liberal left, Al Sharpton has promised to have lawyers at every polling location in Florida in November to ensure no one is denied the right to vote. As well, he promises they will keep their eyes open for abuses.

It is time we reach a new level of consciousness where we come to know that a certain politician or political party is not going to take us to the place we need to get to. The place where war, terrorism, poverty, and other horrific issues cease to exist. It is time to come to the realization that the problems that affect us all are not political. They are spiritual. Voting for either candidate won't change a thing until every individual goes through an inner change.

This past weekend, I had the honor of attending a very special event. His Holiness, The Dalai Lama, spiritual leader of the Buddhist religion came to

South Florida on a speaking tour. He visited Nova Southeastern University, The Office Depot Center and The University of Miami. In his talk entitled "World Peace through Inner Peace," he described the consciousness that I'm talking about. He spoke of the ways we must change if we are to achieve world peace and well being amongst *all* people. What he shared about had nothing to do with political solutions to healing the problems in our world. He spoke of things such as the need for compassion, forgiveness, "inner disarmament" and the promotion of human value.

In conclusion, it is my hope that those who consider themselves staunch conservatives or devout liberals will drop their political weapons and come to a higher place of understanding and consciousness. We are in need of an entire transformation from our current political system and its false promises. It is time for an awakening of a spiritual kind which can't be found on the right or the left. It can only be found in the center. The center of our hearts that is.

CHAPTER 4

Race
and
Culture

Less Than or Less Than?

I had never given much thought to the word "minorities" up until recently. Since the One Planet United column is dedicated to bringing awareness to the harmful effects of prejudice and division among human beings, the word minorities and its meaning has been brought into my consciousness at a deeper level. The more I pay attention, the more I hear the word minorities used when a reference to a certain group of people is mentioned.

When you hear the word minorities, what is the first thing that comes into your mind? Do you think of a group of people that is at a disadvantage in some way from normal everyday people in society? I can't say for certain but I imagine the word was first used to refer to any group that was less in number than another group. The American Heritage dictionary defines the meaning of the word minority as, "The smaller in number of two groups forming a whole." The fact that there are more heterosexual people on the planet than homosexual, if you were counting in number only, you could say that a homosexual was a minority. It could also be referred in the same way to Afro-American, Hispanic and other people who are not considered "Caucasian" that they too could be referred to as minority groups because they are less in number. Some even include women as a minority but if it is in terms of numbers only, I have read that there are more women than men alive on the earth.

Unfortunately, I feel this word has taken on a new meaning and a negative one at that. Today when you hear a group referred to as a minority group, it always seems like it is being used to refer to a group being *less than in value* rather than *less than in number.*

It seems sometimes when I hear the word, the person using it is referring to a group that is of less importance or is less deserving as a human being. If it was being used only as a reference for which group was smaller in number, it would not have a negative effect, but it seems that it is most often used to make one group of less value than the one it is being compared to. The groups most often referred to as minorities are women, gays and lesbians, and blacks and Hispanics. Certainly men and women are different than one another but is one better than the other? Are straight people of more value than gay and lesbian people? Is a white person more important or better than a black or Hispanic person?

As I think back on my own life, I have to say that many of the people who gave me inspiration, wisdom and guidance would be classified as minorities. I have been blessed in my life that when I was going through hard times, periods of indecision and not knowing what to do next, there were always people in my life that were there for me, many being minorities. From personal help for me and my family as well as spiritual direction and growth, some of my most profound insights have come from "minorities."

I bring this topic to the OPU column only to ask that we always think about the words we use and the meanings that we attach to them. In this case, if we use the word "minorities" with the underlying meaning being that we are considering someone less than we are, we've truly lost focus of the value and equality of all people. Minorities? Hey, we're all human beings.

A Global Culture

Have you ever noticed the many sub-cultures within our culture? Every where I look, I see groups of people that separate themselves from others by being a part of a sub-culture. What do I mean by a sub-culture? I guess it could be described as a group of people that hold the same kind of thought, hold the same beliefs and behave in mostly the same way. It seems as if people need to find a sub culture to fit into so they can feel secure and have a feeling that they belong to something. It probably goes all the way back to elementary school when you first realized that you wanted to fit in and be accepted. The alternative to not finding a place to fit in meant that you would be all alone and that was something that was pretty frightening.

Well, as adults, it looks to me that we are still living with the same need to find a group where we fit. That in itself is not a bad thing, but what we have to watch out for is when the group we embrace excludes anyone who doesn't believe as we do.

These groups or as I call them, sub cultures are everywhere around us. Do you notice them? I'll list some that I see. MTV and Hip-Hop, Patriotism, New Age, Recovery, Christianity, Judaism and other religions. How about fans of sports teams, people who ride a certain brand of motorcycle or those who wear the most popular designer clothes? How about the group that idolizes the late Dale Ernhardt? Would you think the company with the swoosh is a subculture? How about certain rock bands like The Grateful Dead or The Rolling Stones? Go to one of their concerts and you are sure to see a sub-culture.

If I embrace the American flag, does it reach a point that I don't know that there are 189 other nations in the world? Even though you love your country can you feel united with all the other nations of our world? If I wear designer clothes displaying the words or initials, DKNY, Guess, Tommy, or RL, do I somehow feel a little better than others? If I just happen to enjoy riding a motorcycle for the feeling of being out in the open air, am I somewhat flawed because I'm not riding a Harley? If I embrace a different spiritual or religious path than the one you have chosen, does that mean that I am not on the true path? By embracing a certain sub-culture, it once again can turn into an "us vs. them" mentality, and that is the kind of belief system that is at the heart of many of our ills in society today. By dividing ourselves into groups, one better than the other, we cannot grasp any feeling or knowing that we are all first brothers and sisters sharing a human experience.

The culture that we could all embrace so as not to divide ourselves from others, would be a global culture. This is the mission of One Planet United. To be a culture that does not exclude anyone. This is the culture that says there are no subcultures because we are all the same. We are human beings who all breathe the same air and have the same needs.

One Planet United doesn't believe that it is wrong to find a group or sub-culture where you might fit in and feel accepted. It is a human need to feel a part of something and have a sense of belonging. Where we need to keep our highest thought though is that we already belong to the human family, and we shouldn't get too obsessed with fitting in, especially at the expense of making others feel excluded or less than. Because we are alive and sharing the planet with our fellow human beings, we already belong to the greatest group there is. It is called the human race.

"Yea, But They're Not Americans"

All I can say is WOW! And all I can do is continue to hope and pray that the prejudice and hatred some hold in their hearts for others will continue to soften as we as a society continue to become more enlightened. In the meantime, we have a lot of work to do.

The wow I am referring to is my reaction from an incident that happened last week during a typical day while I was working with a group of people who were holding a golf tournament for their organization. I spend some of my time each week helping organizations put on golf tournaments mostly for fundraising purposes and organizational gatherings. The group this day was the Latin Chamber of Commerce from Broward County who were holding a tournament for 150 golfers followed by an awards dinner.

The clubhouse is hard to find for many first time visitors so I decided to drive from the entrance of the club to the clubhouse which is about two miles away and post signs on the road with arrows leading to the clubhouse to help keep golfers from getting lost. As I pulled over to post a sign at a four way stop, a very pleasant looking middle aged woman pulled up along side of me and said "Hi, are you selling your condo?" I responded "No, I'm just putting out directional signs for the Latin Chamber of Commerce. They're having a big tournament here today" She then said to me "They're all Spanish huh?" I replied that they were mostly from Argentina, Brazil and other places in South America. To my surprise her next comment in a very stern voice was "Well, I've had enough of THEM." I was kind of stunned that in the space of 20 seconds, our dialogue had reached this point. I responded "but they're all human beings." Here's where the wow comes in. As she was about to drive off, her closing remark to me was, "Yea, but they're not Americans. Have a nice day" At that moment she firmly stepped on her gas pedal and sped off down the road.

I was rather stunned that this whole dialogue took place in a thirty second period of time and how much hatred a simple innocent looking woman could be carrying in her heart. I relayed this story to a very good friend of mine and he kind of chuckled saying that I seem to find myself in many of these kinds of conversations with people. He wanted to know if I have a skill in bringing out peoples true feelings about things. I said, "Hey man, I was just minding my own business on a beautiful sunny day and this woman chose to let her feelings be known how she feels about certain groups of people.

If I had to pick the main reason why I write this column, it is to expose certain ways of thinking that many people follow that keep us from being a united people. This incident just seemed a good fit to pass along as an example.

Unfortunately though, this woman is carrying around hatred in her heart for a "group" of people. She had no idea who the people were that were hosting this golf tournament. She did not get an opportunity to meet them all individually and to find out anything about them as people. She had it in her mind that it was a group that she knows only as "Those People" which eliminates any possibility that she could ever find out that they are just people like the rest of us.

From a personal standpoint, I work with every kind of group you can think of that is putting on a golf tournament either to raise funds for a charity or an organization. My experience working with the golf committee from the Latin Chamber of Commerce was a total joy. I spent the day with some of the nicest people I've ever met and worked with while running a tournament. I only wish that this woman I had met earlier in the day at the four way stop had the opportunity to meet these people she so much despised.

So what can be learned from this short dialogue that I experienced? How about: Is it possible to have an opinion, either good or bad, about a group of people without meeting the individuals within that group? This kind of disease in the hearts of human beings will keep us from ever truly coming to a place of loving our neighbor, which is where we all must get to if we are to live in a peaceful world. If we continue to look at those who are not just like us as "Those People," we will never come close to being a united people.

Unfortunately, this woman who I had this short little dialogue with will probably continue to harbor hatred in her heart for this group and many others. What's more, her statement of ignorance that "they are not Americans" is only in her mind. Every person that was playing in this tournament that day was an American citizen and a productive member of our society. After spending the day with the entire group and having the opportunity to get to know a lot of them personally, I'm happy to say I never saw them as Latino's *or* Americans. I only saw them as fellow human beings.

Observation from a Child

It often amazes me when I encounter a child that seems to be enlightened beyond their years. I sometimes think maybe reincarnation is for real when I hear a child speak as if they are an "old soul." Maybe these children have lived many lifetimes and are far more aware of many things that adults often don't see. I first became aware of an old soul named Mattie Stepanek who recently passed away at the age of twelve from a rare form of cystic fibrosis. Mattie was a published author whose poems about world peace and a united humanity touched many people around the world.

I received an email this past week from another twelve year old. Her name is Ara. She wanted to share a poem she had written that she felt was in strong alignment with One Planet United's mission. I read her poem and her description of where she drew her inspiration from and was so moved that I wanted to share it in today's column. Ara said her inspiration came when she was glancing at a map of the world. As far as I know, it does not have a title:

The seas portray barriers to stop peace from flowing;
But the present peace should be water as well as all of earth,
Unifying itself upon its brothers and sisters
And from there on will only be united,
Human to human,
Not country to country or race to race.

In her words she said "When I was looking at the map, I saw land masses and sea masses. A thought in my mind at the time was about national patriotism and how many countries are so proud of their country. Well, why can't people be proud about the world as one?"

She went on to say, "In my poem, the seas are blocking the countries pride and peace from flowing to everyone. If that peace was spread, it would reach the goal of world peace or in my poems metaphor, it would reach the goal of being one big family."

Incredible words from such a young person but very much at the same time, such an old soul. Ara speaks of the same vision as One Planet United and the awareness that all people must reach if peace in our world is to become a reality. Her words describe a belief that we must rid ourselves from which is that we are separate from others that belong to different "groups" than we do. This belief keeps us from embracing all people as part of one human family.

This answer to peace in our world seems so simple that even some young children "get it." It has nothing to do with who we put in the White House or how much money we spend defending ourselves from "our enemies." It comes down to a radical change pointed out by our young poet, Ara. That is, to remove all barriers and become united not by country or race or political party or sexual orientation or financial status but by our humanity.

Thank you Ara for sharing your enlightenment and wisdom with us. You have a lot to teach us.

Imagine; If You Will

Imagine there's no heaven, it's easy if you try. No hell below us, above us only sky. Imagine all the people, living for today … Imagine there's no countries, it isn't hard to do. Nothing to kill or die for, no religion too. Imagine all the people living life in peace … Imagine no possessions, I wonder if you can. No need for greed or hunger, a brotherhood of man. Imagine all the people, sharing all the world … You may say I'm a dreamer, but I'm not the only one. I hope some day you will join us, and the world will live as one.

A few months back, I wrote a column in honor of the 20th Anniversary of the song "We Are the World." It was a song that moved the hearts of all who heard it. The message was that it was time to reach out and help our neighbors in need and a call to see ourselves as all being a part of one united family; the family of humanity.

Today's column is about another song that has a powerful message as well and has been recorded by dozen's of artists since it first came out over 30 years ago. It is called "Imagine" and was written by John Lennon. I have to admit, until the past few years, I always listened to it with an appreciative ear and thought it was just kind of a "cool" song that had a nice melody.

I never really listened to the words as I have recently. I have begun to see that the lyrics to this song contain a very profound message. Some would scoff, saying that John Lennon was just an old time hippie who spent most of his time high on pot and in his own world of extravagance. I agree he was a different kind of guy, but if you think about it, some of the most unusual people that are now gone have left a mark of profound meaning and importance on the world. I think individuals like Mohandas Gandhi, Albert Einstein, Johan Sebastian Bach and many others who have brought meaning and joy to our lives can be considered as being a little different, but they too left a mark on the world.

After looking at the lyrics in a much deeper way, I believe the song "Imagine" contains truths that, as we continue to evolve as a society, seem to make more and more sense. From one perspective, the words might seem like blasphemy. What do you mean no heaven, no countries, no religion, and no possessions? Isn't this what makes the world function as it does? If John was alive today spreading this message, he would surely meet with serious confrontation.

But what do you think he was really saying? Here is some of the wisdom I gain from his words. First, life is to be lived in the present moment. If we are always living for the future whether it is for security in this life or the next, we will most likely miss the kingdom that is here and now that Jesus so often spoke of. Next, because we have drawn lines and borders all around the world and called them states and countries, a deep division has been created amongst human beings. It's quite an incredible sight when you see a photo or video shot of planet earth taken from space and notice that there are no lines or borders. We have drawn those ourselves and we need to see the problems these lines have created that keep us from seeing all people as our brothers and sisters. I don't think John's call for no religion meant the end of spirituality. He was calling for the end of wars, violence and struggle *in the name of religion*. Finally, if we did not have the obsession and disease to accumulate more and more possessions, would we not think more of what the needs are of those people less fortunate than we are?

I guess you'll have to include me as a dreamer along with John, because I have hope that one day the world *will* live as one. This is the mission of One Planet United and the reason the organization exists. We are trying to bring awareness, enlightenment and healing to all division in the world. We want to be a part of bringing the brotherhood and sisterhood of all people into reality where we can all live in peace.

So I close by saying that I hope someday, if you haven't already, you will join us. It will take a radical shift in consciousness and an ability to embrace the lyrics of this profound song. Imagine if you will, a brotherhood of all human beings living life in peace, sharing all the world and living for today. Sounds pretty good to me. How about you?

Stand Up For Rosa

Today's column is a tribute to a very special human being and one of my all time heroes. I'm talking about Rosa Parks who changed the course of history with one simple act of courage. Rosa passed away on October 24th at the age of 92.

The year was 1955 when at the age of 42, she committed an act of defiance that changed the course of American History and earned her the title, "the mother of the civil rights movement." At that time in history, segregation of blacks and whites was in full swing. Much of the racial discrimination was legally sanctioned which kept blacks out of certain jobs and neighborhoods. Restaurants, bathrooms, drinking fountains and the like were clearly marked with signs that said "whites only" or "colored only." Despite rules requiring blacks to yield their seats to whites on public buses, Ms. Parks refused to give her seat to a white man which got her arrested but at the same time, started a revolution.

What also resulted from Ms. Park's act of courage was that a small town minister from Montgomery, Alabama named Martin Luther King Jr. got behind her cause and took it to the masses. Dr. King has always been known as the founder of the modern Civil Rights Movement but many believe that without Ms. Park's initiation, things would not have unfolded in the same way. Actually, many do not know that Ms. Parks was active for many years trying to heal race relations and her action that particular day was certainly not a "spur of the moment" decision.

Was this little lady of courage important to our society as a whole? By a unanimous vote of congress she became the first woman to lie in honor in the Capitol Rotunda in Washington, D.C. where thousands of people lined up to file past her coffin and say thank-you. Since the great humanitarian Henry Clay in 1852, only 29 other national leaders have been given this honor. They include Abraham Lincoln, John F. Kennedy and most recently, Ronald Reagan.

In my last column, I was pointing out that it seems that a majority of the population is infatuated with celebrities as well as those in the nightly news that are making headlines mostly for acts of impropriety. To reach a higher consciousness, we need to replace our celebrity heroes with heroes such as Ms. Parks. We need to emulate her voice and stance of courage to speak out about things that repress certain groups of people and where the superiority of any group of people is festering and growing.

Ms. Parks can teach us all to be more courageous and stand up when we see and experience situations and things that we know are wrong. Her example can give us the courage to interrupt someone when they are telling an inappropriate joke. Her example can make us speak up when we see someone being abused rather than just looking the other way and saying it is none of our business. Her example can inspire us to speak out against prejudice when we see it whether it be racial, religious, political or any other mode of thinking where superiority claims are promoted.

So we say to you Rosa, "You Go Girl." Go and rest in peace and we say thank you for your courage and the lessons you have taught us all. You are a true hero and an example that we all need to follow to help us become a united people and a united planet where hatred, bigotry, and prejudice do not exist. We honor you, we thank you and we bless you.

"Listen, Can You Hear The Sound?"

The purpose of the One Planet United column has always been to try to bring awareness to the things all people share in common as well as expose the harm that is often caused when we mostly see differences in others. I'm talking about differences that bring about prejudice, intolerance and suspicion of people because of their skin color, social class, religious beliefs and the like.

Along that line of thinking, I became aware of a powerful insight that once again, told me that at the core of our existence, we are all the same. This new realization came one morning this past week when I was in the hospital for a second time trying to find relief from a ten year old condition I have had that inhibits the full use of my left arm.

For this particular procedure, I had to be put under anesthesia. As the preparation began, I was met by four different nurses who all had a part in making sure that everything was ready when the doctor arrived to perform the actual procedure. The first nurse welcomed me with a bright smile and said she was going to prep my IV as well as take my blood pressure and temperature. She also placed a small clamp on the end of my index finger that was connected to a heart monitor that radiated the sound of my heart beating.

As I lay there alone, I was suddenly struck by the sound of my own heartbeat. At this moment, I began to think of the words of a song that a friend had shared with me in the past week, which pointed out that the thing all people have most in common is that we all have a heartbeat that works exactly the same. The words to the first verse say;

"Listen, can you hear the sound? Hearts beating, all the world around. Down in the valley, out on the plain. Everywhere around the world, a heartbeat sounds the same. Black or white, red or tan, it's the heart of the family of man. Whoa, it's beatin away, Whoa, it's beatin away."

I came to the realization of how profound the words to this song were. Then as each nurse came to do what they were to do to get me ready, I shared my insight with each of them. What made it more amazing was that each of the nurses was a different nationality and originally came from a different place in the world. By their accents and the way they looked, it was easy to tell that they were from assorted places and backgrounds. I inquired where each was from and they told me; Ireland, Grenada, France, and Pittsburgh, Pa. It made me think that no matter whose finger was attached to this monitor, regardless of nationality, sex, race, religious affiliation, political beliefs, etc., the sound would still be the same.

Through this experience, I was reminded once again, that at the core (heart) of all human beings, we are very much the same. We all have hearts that beat to keep us alive and those are the same hearts that can help us see the beauty of all people that we are sharing our human experience with.

A thought to ponder; The next time you might want to find a reason to separate yourself from someone who is "different" than you are, know that at the deepest place, your beating hearts sound exactly the same and join you together as members of the same human family.

And the Child Shall Lead Them

Maybe my friend is right. When it comes to prejudice attitudes that are embedded in many adults, it might be the children that are going to teach them how wrong they are. My thoughts come from a conversation I was having with a friend, telling him how much it hurts when I see parents openly speaking of their prejudices in front of their own children. When I experience this scenario, it makes me believe that one more generation will be infected with the perceptions and the attitudes of their caretakers.

An example of this took place a few weeks ago when I found myself at a function that included parents and their children. When the topic came to schools, one of the mothers blurted out, "I don't want my son going to XYZ High School because I want him to know that he's white and not black." Her ongoing comments were making me cringe and I thought about how her son, who was sitting right next to her, was hearing this. I did my best to keep my opinions and comments to myself for I did not want to turn this special occasion into a possible heated debate.

The dialogue continued for a few more minutes when a man who was also seated at our table joined in the discussion. He boldly blurted out that he has already informed his daughter that if she ever came home with a black person, he would disown her. I took a moment to ask him how old his daughter was and he said she was nine. He continued to bring up people from other races he had issues with so I asked, "How do you feel about the human race?" He did not really know how to answer my question. Upon overhearing his comments, his wife leaned over to me and my wife and with an embarrassed grin said, "He's really a white supremacist." I was feeling a strong degree of tension and unrest but knew it was not the appropriate time to engage in a discussion about prejudice. What I was thinking was that this little nine year old girl was being programmed by parents that were adamant about their prejudice beliefs.

As I shared the aches of my heart with my friend about this experience, he said that he believes going forward, maybe it's going to be children teaching parents about many things, prejudice included. We were in agreement in our belief that children are often the one's that in today's world are more evolved in their consciousness. It gave me hope to hear his insights. He went on to say that he believes we will one day soon reach a place were a child will say to their parent, "Mom/Dad, why don't you like the family that moved in next door? You don't even know them." We were also in agreement that many of the things that parents are learning these days often come from their kids, so why not about prejudice and bigotry. An example my friend thought of was recycling. It has been children who have educated their parents on the benefits that recycling brings to the environment.

If you think about, there are many other things that children have been learning and passing along to their parents. How about the harmful effects of smoking? You would think that parents are the ones educating their kids on this subject, but in many cases, it's the other way around. When my daughter was little she never missed an opportunity to remind her grandmother every time she lit up a cigarette that she was harming herself as well as those around her. The same goes for the use of alcohol. I was with a woman last week that told me that after 20 years of alcoholic drinking, her 8 year old daughter's comment brought her to her bottom. The little girl walked into the kitchen at the same time she was taking a hit off a quart bottle of gin. She looked up at her mom and said, "Mommy, don't drink that. Alcohol is a drug." That simple phrase jolted the mother so deeply that it was the catalyst that made her seek treatment. It is also the reason she has been clean and sober for more than 10 years.

So I close with two suggestions. First, let us be extremely careful what attitudes and beliefs we are passing along to our children especially when it comes to our own prejudice and intolerance. Second, let's stay open to what our children can teach us about what they know is right in the world. Sometimes, they can be our greatest teachers.

An Old Saying

What's the old saying? If I remember correctly, it goes like this. "You can't judge a book by its cover." I guess it depends on the generation you grew up in, as to how often you heard it. I know from my generation, it was heard all the time.

If we don't happen to hear it as much today, is it something we still should pay attention to? I'll share a recent personal story that says that the answer is a powerful yes!

A few weeks ago on a Sunday evening, I had pulled up to the pump at my local gas station to fill up for the week ahead. At the moment I began to pump the gas into my car, I suddenly felt the ground begin to vibrate and soon after the pumps and nozzle were trembling as well. A car had just pulled up to the front and parked in front of the convenience store. The windows to the vehicle were darkened to the point that you could not tell who was inside. The next moment, two young kids got out of the car. The driver went into the store while the passenger remained, leaning up against the car with the door open. The music coming from the thumping car was very loud and the gas station was in full vibration. Here is what happened (only in my mind) in the next 30 seconds.

Since these guys were both black, dressed in hip-hop attire and had the look of nothing but trouble, I went into a fast projection that the fellow who went into the store was going to hold up the cashier while the guy outside was keeping watch. OK, now back to reality. First, I reminded myself that I write a lot about the harm of pre-judging and profiling people we don't know. Next, I decided to confront this "profile" I had made by starting a conversation with the kid that was outside leaning against the car.

I walked over and said, "You know, my mom always told me that if I listen to music that loud, I was going to go deaf." He broke out in a huge smile and said back to me, "Oh, it ain't nothing man. I'll be alright." I quickly learned that the profile I had drawn of this kid as an angry, viscous, potential criminal was what I had created in my mind. He was only a teenager of 17 or 18 years old that was just trying to fit in.

Did I not heed the advice I got as a child about not judging a book by its cover? I guess not at the original moment, but I figured since I write a column about issues regarding prejudice, intolerance and division, I better practice what I preach.

Here's something to think about. Check out your own life and where your mind can go when it comes to pre-judging others before you get to know them. See where fear gets in the way of reaching out to find out about someone before you decide what kind of person they are. It's seems to be a problem for all of us. It will cease to be a problem though if we take our own inventory to see where we might be pre-judging and profiling others before we have had a chance to read the book.

The Lasting Solution

Writing the One Planet United column often inspires readers to respond to my commentary. Sometimes, the feedback is very moving and touches my heart deep at the center while other times, what I have written has struck a nerve that has not sat well with someone and their response back to me is not too warm and friendly. What I like as much as anything is when someone responds by sending me a blurb, a poem or a story that creates inspiration for a new column. Such is the case today.

A few weeks back I received a blurb from someone who said that they wanted to share it with me because it was so much in line with the OPU column as well as the mission of the One Planet United organization. The title is called, "Narrowness" and it was written by a man named Meher Baba. Baba wrote a book back in the 1920's called "God Speaks." What he was most known for was that he was Gandhi's spiritual advisor and mentor. I feel the authors thoughts are a powerful description of where our culture needs to look if we are to eventually live in a world of peace and harmony. I would like to share it with you.

"All narrowness limits love. Humanity is breaking itself into narrow groups based upon caste, creed, race, nationality, religion or culture. All this is due to ignorance, prejudice and selfishness. It can only be mended by fostering a spirit of mutuality which will derive its strength from a sense of the inviolable unity of all life. No line of action can be really fruitful, unless it is in complete harmony with this truth.
As long as a social problem is dominated by the idea of numbers and multiplicity; there is no lasting solution for it. The lasting solution can come only when it is illuminated by the truth of the indivisible totality and intrinsic unity of all. The future of humanity is in the hands of those who share this vision"

What comes across to me is how narrowness breeds mostly in "group think" mentality. What exactly is "group think" consciousness or mentality? I believe it is when a person feels a sense of unity only when they are with their own kind of people whether that is people who worship as they do, vote as they do or for the most part believe in all the same things. It is a fact of life that all people feel a little more secure when they are around "like minded" people, but when one's alignment with people is aligned with only a narrow belief system, unity with all people is not likely to be possible. Baba says that this can be mended by fostering a spirit of mutuality, which means we have to see all people as our equals and worthy of honor and respect.

I feel the ending is the most powerful when Baba says that the future of humanity is in the hands of those who share this vision. How awesome will it be when this is the vision of us all? "A dream" you say? If I look back on my life, I'm happy to say that many of my own dreams have indeed become a reality. Let's keep hoping and praying.

"ET Phone Home"

Illegal immigration and the issues surrounding our current system happen to be at the forefront of today's headlines. I am happy that we are attempting to reform a system that has long been ignored and in need of repair. What bothers me though is that once again, this whole issue for many fuels the belief that it's "Us against Them" and that somehow certain classes of people are more worthy than others. It enhances so many of our relational problems with those who are from a different culture or who live on a different part of our planet. What bothers me as much as anything though is hearing the names used by the media and many others to identify immigrants. You would think they are referring to beings from another planet, not people from another country.

What terminology am I talking about? It is heard more and more in the news these days and it seems to have become a part of everyday language. I'm talking about the term "alien" when it comes to referring to someone from a different country. Most often, the full term that is used is "illegal alien" which seems even stranger. If you went up to someone on the street and asked them where aliens live, most often you would hear the response "in outer space on other planets."

One Planet United envisions a world where there is no such thing as a human being that is referred to as an alien or worse, an illegal alien. I know some will be upset and say that "those people" don't belong here and they should stay in their own country. John Lennon's song "Imagine" has a line that says, "Imagine there's no countries." I believe that was his belief that without borders in the first place, there would not be the concept of "us and them." What if these man made borders that create much division in our world were never created in the first place? Seems to me this would destroy a whole way of thinking that has led many to believe that they are different from "them."

I believe "them" is the same as us and it is time to begin to see all people as members of one human family. I know for many this idea is hard to grasp, but so were many things in our past that seemed impossible to believe and eventually embrace. Such as the evils of slavery and segregation, the equality of men and women, or the dangers of cigarette smoke. What has happened is that we have awakened to a new and higher consciousness in so many of the belief systems we once held onto so tightly.

We are all first and foremost, human beings living on a planet called earth. We are members of the same race. If we are to reach this new height in consciousness, a simple place to start would be in the terminology we use when referring to people from other countries. Foreigners, illegals, aliens? Who are these people really? In reality, they are members of the human family.

So let us begin to see that *all people* are worthy to be called "human beings." Let's do away with any terminology that can be construed as demeaning or derogatory. Remember that immigrants are members of our human family and no less worthy of respect than anyone else. There are 6 billion people on our planet. Look to see the heart of each and every one. When we do, all divisions, indifference and intolerance will magically disappear and unity among all of us will become a reality.

Minorities? We're All Human Beings

The headline in a recent South Florida newspaper read; "How We Are Changing." It was an article describing the results of a recent study that said that the United States is now made up of over 100 million minorities. With approximately 300 million people living in the U.S., the study reveals that one third of the population is made up of minorities. This includes Hispanics, African Americans, Latinos, people from the Middle East and the Far East as well. People now living in the U.S. include those who were originally from places such as Puerto Rico, Japan, Honduras, Haiti, Cuba, Canada, India and the list goes on.

So the question is, how does this make you feel? It is truly amazing that for those that believe that this growth of minorities is a good thing, there seems to be just as many who are "opposed." Those who believe diversity is a good thing welcome the opportunity to mix people from other cultures and races. They want their children to know that "human beings" come in all colors. On the other side of the aisle, the sentiment is not quite the same. A degree of anger and fear seem to live in the hearts of those who do not welcome the idea that the world is changing.

Since I fall in line with the first group, my first suggestion is that we do away with the term "minorities." I believe it this term, when referring to people who are only less in number, creates a feeling in some that people who fall into a class labeled "minority" are 'less than" or "minor" as human beings. When we believe that a group of people (or individual) are less than us because of where they were born or what color their skin happens to be, we set ourselves up first to live in a divided world, but more importantly, to live with a feeling of being superior to others. This type of thinking is what was at the core of the Holocaust and even though in today's modern culture (in the U.S.) we don't go around exterminating those we might believe are "less than" we are, we still often live with the same attitudes. It is these attitudes that keep us from embracing differences in race, religion, culture, sexual orientation and language.

I recently heard a well known radio talk show host say that we should call the word diversity; perversity. He held nothing back in his belief that diversity is a cancer and that tolerance would ultimately be what kills us all. Unfortunately for this man of fear and hate, the world is changing, diversity is continuing to grow and there is not much we can do to change that.

For me, I don't want to change it. When my wife and I moved to South Florida over 14 years ago, we specifically picked a city to settle in where we believed our kids would grow up around other children who were all races, religions and social economic classes. We wanted them to be exposed to a world that was made up of all kinds of people so they would become adults that would respect and honor all people. So far, it seems to have worked very well.

Let's remember that when it comes to the human race, there is no person or group that is minor or less than. We are all equals. We are all members of the same family and when we all one day come to this realization; peace on earth will be close at hand.

CHAPTER 5

Family

A Family Divided—(Part 1)

Today's column addresses a major form of division in our world and that is the division of the family. Many families today are being broken up and fragmented in astronomical numbers. What makes this so painful and such an important issue is that a lot of experts relate the breakup of the family to many of the social ills that exist in today's society. Many people in the field of family therapy tie in things such as crime, suicide, addiction, teenage pregnancy and the like to the breakdown of the family. Although hard to prove in exact numbers, there is evidence that the health of the family in our society has a direct correlation to the health of our world.

This division and breakdown is brought on by so many underlying forces. In this three part series, OPU will address what I feel are the most destructive forces in the breakup of the family. That being, divorce, addiction, and the inability to forgive.

In part one, I want to address divorce and it's crippling effects on the family. In the year 2003 it is noted that 50% of all marriages will end in divorce and unfortunately, a lot of these are beyond repair by the time the couple realizes the damage that has been done.

One Planet United wants to challenge people to stop this huge division in our society by creating what noted author Harville Hendrix calls *The Conscious Marriage*. It is being *unconscious* of what causes division in relationships that can lead to divorce and thus the breakdown of the family. We owe it to our children to let them grow up in a home where two adults that have made a commitment to each other for life, really are *conscious* about how to keep their family together. Too many people are going into marriage with little or no skills on how to keep the relationship growing in a healthy direction. A marriage is a living, breathing organism as are a lot of things and without daily maintenance and tending to, it often dies.

Society in relation to marriage, often plays a role in this division as well. Tell anyone you plan to get married and most often you will hear a laugh or a great deal of skepticism. Comedians often joke about marriage, and television almost never puts a positive light on marriage. Fidelity, one of the main things that keeps a relationship going in the right direction, is not held in very high regard in a lot of media circles. Just tune in talk radio, watch TV or go to a movie, and see how marriage and family are almost never promoted as something good and healthy for our society.

OPU asks all people to become *conscious* of how the division of the human family is at the core of so many problems, and to take responsibility to do all they can in keeping their marriages and families together. Our society will be much better off and our children will grow up to be a lot healthier, both emotionally and spiritually.

A Family Divided—(Part 2)

Today's column is part two of a three part column entitled "A Family Divided". Last time, I addressed the destructive and divisive power of divorce on families and children and the need for parents to begin to have *conscious* marriages. I pointed out the strong need for knowledge of what makes a healthy union between a husband and wife and that a marriage is a living and breathing organism that needs daily maintenance to survive. I also noted that many experts in the field of family therapy say that the health of the family in our society has a direct correlation to the health of our world.

In today's column, One Planet United will address the topic of addiction and its powerful destructive force on a family. Most often, when someone is addicted, it is not visible to most people, except to those in the immediate family. Later on, when its power has begun to cause a lot of damage, it turns into what many families term, "The elephant in the living room." This is the time when all those in the family are keenly aware of the addiction, but too afraid to say anything.

Addiction shows its face in so many ways, most evidently scene in the form of drugs and alcohol. These two forms of addiction alone are responsible for tearing apart and dividing families in astronomical numbers, but there are many more forms of addiction that follow close behind. Being addicted to work, sex, gambling, food, spending or religion can be and often is, as destructive as a drugs or alcohol.

The issue with the person addicted is not the substance or activity that has a hold on them. It is an inner void that must be filled with something that will numb their feelings. Because an addict can only focus on their next "fix", they live a life that hurts those closest to them. From stealing and lying, to never being able to keep a promise, to living a life of secrecy in their own family, this only can mean heartache and destruction for those we love the most and those who love us. I'm not a doctor so I will not attempt to describe the physiological side of addiction. What I want to bring to light is that if you or someone in your family is an addict, you first must be honest enough to see what it is doing to you and your family's life, and second, you must reach out for help. If addiction of any kind is active, whether it's a dad, a mom, or a brother or sister, there will be nothing but destruction and division in the family, and there can be no restoration until the addict surrenders to their problem and reaches out for help.

The good news for the person who is addicted is that there is help. Some find help with family counseling, as well as a renewed commitment to their faith, but the place that statistics say helps the most are 12 Step Programs. The original 12 Step program was Alcoholics Anonymous which started back in 1935, and since then, 12 Step Groups for every known addiction have started and are growing all over the world. These groups are helping millions of people recover and are helping scores of family's be restored to health and wholeness. You can find numbers in the phone book as well as find information on the internet for all 12 Step groups.

Once again, it is my belief that the health of our society is greatly related to the health of our families and if the destructive power of addiction has control, a family cannot survive. If you are in the grips of addiction, be honest and reach out for help. If you do, there is a good chance you and your family will not only survive, but be able to live in a place of peace and harmony beyond your wildest dreams.

A Family Divided—(Part 3)

Today, One Planet United concludes the three part series on the division of the family. In part one, I addressed the division and destruction caused by divorce and the need to nurture marriage as well as challenge people to have a "conscious marriage." The term was introduced by noted marriage therapist, Harville Hendrix, which means to have knowledge of what makes a marital relationship grow and develop in healthy ways, thus keeping families united.

In part two, I talked about the power of addiction to divide and destroy families. Not only addiction to alcohol and drugs, but to work, sex, spending, exercise, food and many other substances and activities. I noted that these powerful forces can tear apart the family and that there is help for anyone, most notably, through 12 Step Programs.

In part three, OPU wants to shed light on one more area of pain and destruction in families today and that is in a person's inability to forgive. Many families today have fathers and/or mothers that stopped talking to their children 10 and 20 years ago. There are families where siblings hold anger and resentment toward each other that goes back for years. Some reasons come from extremely serious issues where a lot of pain was present and others are just simple misunderstandings that became buried and never addressed.

I believe what is at the core and difficulty in our inability to forgive, lies mostly in our own self centeredness and ego. I do believe that some past harm done in families was so destructive that forgiveness would only be possible through divine intervention. As well, I also believe that most anger, resentment, and misunderstanding can be healed. Someone in the family though, must begin the process.

First, begin with the end in mind. Visualize that the relationship with the person or persons in your family that the ties have been severed with is now a loving and healthy relationship. Next, the best way to proceed is to write a handwritten letter stating your desire to heal the pain and separation that exists. Ask if it would be possible to meet in person or by telephone to talk. The process has now begun. To look at it another way, go back once again and begin with the end in mind. Visualize yourself at the last moments of your life and see if it was better to *not* reach out in an effort to reconcile. Many people wait until this time and it is often too late or reality sets in that many fruitful years that might have been, have been lost.

Old pain, hurts and resentments in families are often unspoken misunderstandings that turn into cancers of the spirit. If our children are growing up watching us be bitter, angry and resentful at our own families, remember the famous poem, "Children Learn What They Live." Take a risk, reach out and know that by healing your family relationships, you also help heal our world today and the generations that follow.

CHAPTER 6

Spiritual Self Worth

Surgery for the Soul

Today's column is bound to stir as many emotions as when I write about topics such as religion and politics. The One Planet United view of both religion and politics usually stirs strong feelings either in favor of, or opposition to, my personal views. To be quite honest, I'd rather write about things that are warm and fuzzy so I didn't have to experience some of the emails from those who disagree. What I write about each week is sometimes controversial, but my goal is only to get people to think at a deeper level, so here goes.

Today I want to address the myth that a person will become much happier by altering their appearance through plastic surgery. It's a big lie and I'm pleading with you not to "buy in." The advertisements are taking over newspapers and magazines and have to be a close second to the car and truck industry in the frequency that you will see them. The first thing you might notice is that the term plastic surgery has been changed to "cosmetic surgery." From the practitioners in some of the recent ads I have come across in the local paper, here is what you are being told;

Dr. _____ raises plastic surgery to a new level of art. "Come meet real life makeovers at our upcoming "free" workshop." Seating is limited.
Dr. _____ says, "Look your best without looking artificial."
Dr. _____ says, "Looking Better, Feeling Better, Confidence, Self Esteem ... That's what it's all about." Come for a "free" seminar.
Dr. _____ says, "Looking your age has become a thing of the past."

And further, here is what you are being sold. The list of available procedures is growing and the names they have been given are quite exotic. Heard of any of these? Three Dimensional Space Lift, Quick Recovery Breast Augmentation, Lip Selection, Boot by Allergen, Dermawave and Skin Station, 3-D Buttockplasty, Impolite, Thermage Skin Tightening, Tummy Tucks, Wrinkle Fillers, Body Sculpting, FRAXEL Laser, Minimal Incision Facelifts, Arm Lifts, Neck lifts, Eyelid Lifts, Neck Liposuction, Mesotherapy, Alloderm, Restylane, Perlane, Radiance, Fat Grafting, Mini Facial Liposuction, Lipografting—Facial Sculpting, Radiesse, Customized Peels, and Anti-Aging Therapy. (I find it interesting that most of these procedures listed come up on my spell check as "not in dictionary.") Also, many of these doctors are running specials if you "act now," you won't miss out in maintaining a "youthful" appearance.

Here's the lie I believe you are being asked to buy into. You are being led to believe that by altering your outsides, you will change your insides. You are also being told that getting older is a bad and shameful thing and that you can stop or stall the aging process. If you are a young female, you are being sold the lie that who you are is all about how you look on the outside.

From a different perspective, here are a few of my feelings on the subject. First, from the physical viewpoint. Plastic surgery is unnatural, invasive to the body and can end in death. It can have serious side effects and often causes auto-immune disorders, infections and permanent scarring. It is known that over 50% of all people who have plastic surgery go back again because they are not happy with the initial procedure.

Maybe by now you are asking, how does this subject fit the One Planet United perspective? It is my belief that the more we become divided from ourselves, the more we become divided from one another. When I say divided from ourselves, I mean that I feel that who we are as human beings has nothing to do with our outer appearance and that the more we buy into the myth that this is false, the further from our true selves we become.

I am also writing about this today because I want to offer an alternative suggestion for anyone considering plastic surgery as the answer to their inner unhappiness. My hope is that you will put off cutting up your body or injecting it with "miracle youth potions" and try something else first. Here is my suggestion. Take the money you would have spent and the normal 1–2 week recovery time that is often needed and go away to a retreat center that focuses on "sculpting your soul." Here it is possible that you will find the fulfillment that you were hoping to achieve at the hands of a plastic surgeon who, keep in mind, is often motivated by profit. While on retreat, you will be put in the hands of "spiritual surgeons" whose focus is on your inner beauty and your true self. When you go internally to this place and meet the "you" that comes from your soul, you will know that true happiness comes from within. When you return, many will notice how different you "look" on the outside, but it won't be because your outer appearance was surgically altered. It will be because your soul, the person you truly are, will be shining and portraying the true beauty that lies within us all.

Seventeen and a Half

Last week I found myself at an unplanned visit to my doctor's office to be evaluated for any possible injuries due to being part of a four car accident. As the police report stated, I was vehicle number two that was rear ended by vehicle number one. The force of vehicle number one hitting vehicle number two crashed vehicle number two into vehicle number three which then lightly impacted vehicle number four. The good news is that no one was hurt although vehicle number one and two had to be towed from the scene.

While trying to pass some time for my usual lengthy wait in the doctor's office, I scanned the magazine rack for something to read. My eyes caught a recent copy of SEVENTEEN magazine. I pulled it from the rack because I wanted to see if anything had changed in the past four years as to the messages that this magazine was selling to teenagers. It brought me back to a time five or six years ago when my daughter who was 15 at the time and I were on an airplane flight across the country. There happened to be a copy of SEVENTEEN magazine in the seat pocket that she had pulled out and had begun to look through. As I glanced over her shoulder to see what the content was that she was reading, I couldn't help but use the time as a teachable moment. Since we had five hours to kill, I asked my daughter if she would humor me for a few minutes. I asked her to start on the first page and go through every page all the way to the end and see how many articles or advertisements had to do with a girls outsides versus her insides. We saw advertisements that covered it all on the outside that included shampoos, mascara and eyeliners, lip gloss and lip sticks, skin crèmes, deodorants, acne creams, and perfumes. Articles and other advertisements were focused on Hollywood celebrities, teenage heartthrobs, romance and the latest "hot" trends in designer clothes. The SEVENTEEN I was flipping through this past week had all the latest information on Hillary Duff, Jessica Simpson, Nick Carter and adorning the cover was Ashley Simpson. The stories on the cover included 260 plus hair and makeup tricks; get a dancers body; figure fixers for your thighs, arms, tummy, legs and hips.

My reason for making these observations in today's column is because I believe the messages that are being sent in most all media fall closely in line with my description of the topics and ads in SEVENTEEN magazine. If you are a regular reader of the One Planet United column, you know that the main focus is to look on the inside of yourself as well as others. With the bombardment of outward focus that young people are fed on a day to day basis, is it possible that they will know that their character is significantly more important than the way they look on the outside? I know this sounds like I think that teens should forget about their appearance and work on developing character and the ability to see the good in others. I'm not saying that. What I am saying is that there needs to be a balance, which I currently don't see.

In the issue I was referring to that I picked up last week, there was a two page column on how young people celebrate their faith and another story about a 20 year old girl who was dying from cancer. These "inside" issues took up only a total of 5 pages. What caught my attention was that the focus on the outside was so out of balance with the focus on the inside.

What I'm hoping and advocating is that parents take those times for teachable moments when it comes to the important things in life like caring for others, growing spiritually and developing character. My fear is that a lot of Mom's are the one's that are buying this kind of magazine for their teenage daughters because they want them to fit in and be popular.

What I want to do is encourage young people to come to a higher place. A place you could call Seventeen and a Half. Instead of seeing life through the eyes of the editors of SEVENTEEN magazine, I want to encourage teens to see life more through the eyes of that internal place inside themselves that enhances self love and solid inner qualities. If they do, the focus on their outer appearance and their fascination with the lives of celebrities will take on significantly less meaning and thus a healthy balance of inside and out will prevail. This inward and outward balance can only mean a healthier society overall.

Fitness—Inside *and* Out

We live in an age where physical beauty and physical fitness are the main focus in so many people's lives. It seems to border on obsession. Everywhere you look, the media is pounding away at the message that you can be prettier, skinnier, or have bigger muscles and a streamlined physique. Health club ads are everywhere, encouraging us to sign up and get fit. From the magazines in supermarkets to the ads in newspapers and on TV, we are bombarded with messages that make us feel flawed if we are not paying attention to the way we look, particularly on the outside.

In today's column, One Planet United is addressing the issue of fitness. Only, we will ask the question; is fitness only physical? If you are into fitness, does that mean that you jog 5 miles a day or go to the gym and work out 3 times each week? OPU believes that being fully fit as a human being includes more than physical workouts and conditioning. It is the belief that the spiritual part of our make up needs consistent workouts and conditioning also. To be complete, whole, and fully alive as a human being, their needs to be a balance between stretching our muscles, and stretching our spirits

Many people think nothing of spending 2 hours a day, 3 to 4 times per week at their neighborhood fitness club, or waking up an hour early to run 3 miles. This is not a bad thing by any means and the commitment it takes should be admired. On the other hand, the thought of taking 15 minutes each morning to pray, meditate or read something to give our souls a workout to start the day, is something a lot of people would never consider. Unfortunately for this fact, a lot is missed because of it.

When we work out physically, there really is only one beneficiary and that is ourselves. Our bodies will look better, our stamina will be better and our cardio vascular system will strengthen. When we work out spiritually, *we* benefit greatly, but so do those around us. People in our families, our communities and our world benefit when we take the time individually to strengthen our spiritual muscles. When we take the time to quiet our souls and ask the God of our understanding to show us the ways of peace and compassion, the whole world benefits. If we ask to be shown ways we can be kinder or gentler to those around us, the benefits fall on many, and not just ourselves.

I am not saying that we trade our physical workouts for spiritual workouts. I'm only suggesting that when we pay as much attention to our spiritual conditioning as we do our physical conditioning, more change for good in our world will happen. Our souls begin to transform so that we see the souls of others, thus making us feel more at peace with our selves and our neighbors.

Can you imagine what our planet would be like if every person alive spent just 15 minutes each day in prayer and meditation, asking that they be shown the way of love in all situations in their daily lives? Could their be prejudice, hatred and division? Why not try it for 30 days and see what changes take place in your *inner* life?

On a closing note, if you are already one who meditates an hour a day, don't forget that your body needs attention too. It might be time for you to take a brisk walk.

Extreme Makeover from The Inside

I had often thought about writing a column on today's topic but felt that it's one more of the things in this world that I'm powerless to change and by writing about it, I would just make myself more frustrated. I now think that if I purge my thoughts and feelings on the subject, maybe then I can just let it go. I'm certainly not going to change what's happening in this area, but I can't help expressing my frustration, anger and disappointment that this issue is alive and growing.

I'm talking about the cosmetic surgery industry. At a breakneck speed, the industry is pouring more and more money into advertising letting you know that they have the ability to take the disappointment you feel about yourself and your appearance and bring about "a new you." I guess the inspiration to finally put my thoughts on paper came when I received a card in the mail this week from the dermatologist's office that my family has used over the past 10 years stating that they now are offering cosmetic surgery to their patient services. Now as well as being able to treat teenage acne and potentially hazardous moles, they are offering the following. Botox, wrinkle removal, tummy tucks, liposuction, lip rejuvenation, facelifts, hair replacements and many other treatments with names you would need a medical expert to define. I did not see the availability of have a breast enlargement, but of course that is available at most of your downtown cosmetic surgery centers. I was looking through an insert in our local newspaper and counted nine different advertisements from local doctors competing to alter your body each with such catchy phrases such as: "I'm 49, a teacher, married 23 years, raised 3 children, and it shows" or "Why not look as young as you feel?" There was one advertisement from a female plastic surgeon that had the question "Who do you want to inject your botox? It was implying that a woman doctor can be trusted more than a man when it comes to doing it right.

Oh well, back to my angst and disappointment. It is coming from this being one more way that we avoid looking at ourselves from the inside first and the outside last. The obsession with our physical appearance keeps us further and further from the truth of who we really are. The body that houses our soul is really nothing more than a casing that houses our true self and it seems that the more we are attracted to altering how we look on the outside(physical), the less we focus upon our inside(soul.) The frustration comes from the fact that this idea of "happiness through cosmetic surgery" is being sold to us and a lot of people are buying it. If that is so, than this means we are looking further and further from where true happiness and contentment lies and that is on the inside.

Think about the message we are passing along to our children when our main focus is on our physical appearance and not on our inner being. As we age, we can't really control (only alter for a brief time) the process of the physical changes our bodies will go through but we can control how our soul will age. That's where our kids need to see us enhancing our lives and deepening our relationship with our inner selves. Think back to when you were graduating from high school and maybe you were lucky that you had parents that wanted to reward you with a graduation gift for this great achievement and milestone. Do you remember what the gift was that you received? Was it a new car perhaps or maybe a special trip in your honor? Possibly a new wardrobe or a gift of cash? Some folks find it hard to believe when I tell them that two of my daughter's classmates that graduated with her three years ago received money for breast enlargements. These girls were 18 years old! I wonder if I'm the only one who is a little outraged and bewildered at parents who would embrace this idea.

The more obsessed we are with how we look and the more we buy into the belief that altering our appearance will bring happiness, the further we get from knowing the true source of inner peace and contentment which is on the inside in our souls and in our hearts. True and authentic beauty does not come from the size of your body parts, the amount of wrinkles you do or don't have or how much hair you have on your head. It comes from your soul. I often have the opportunity to meet, work and spend time with elderly folks who are way beyond the vanity years. What I often see is an "inner beauty" that can only be seen through their eyes.

If you are a steady reader of the One Planet United column, you might be asking how this topic ties into the OPU message. That being to try to expose and breakthrough any division in our world. The division I am addressing today is of the deepest and most subtle of all and that is being divided from oneself. In all things, where there is division, there is little chance for peace. When outward looks and appearance become our obsession, we have become very much divided from our true selves, and the hopes of true inner peace as well.

CHAPTER 7

Raising
The Collective
Consciousness

Equality Is On the Rise

Is it possible that we will have a black president in January of 2009? Or possibly a woman? Or maybe a Mormon? These possibilities excite me, not because I'm rooting for a particular candidate but that it verifies to me that the consciousness of humanity is continuing to grow in the right direction. What I mean by this is that regardless of your race, gender, sexual orientation or religious beliefs more than ever before, the idea of equality is becoming a reality and that no matter who you are, you have an equal chance with everyone else to be or do whatever you desire.

Of course this is not how it always was and we're not totally there yet but we're on the right path. It was only a short time ago that African Americans were owned as personal property and society agreed that this was totally acceptable. A little more recently, when it was time to cast your vote for the next President of the United States, if you were a woman, you were not invited to join in. You stayed home.

Although racial and sexual divides still exist and we have a ways to go, there is evidence continually coming forth that shows that we are evolving in the right direction. It might come as a shock to many of us to realize that there has not been a "white" "male" secretary of state in Washington for the past 12 years. Condoleezza Rice is currently serving and was preceded by Colin Powell from 2001–2005 and Madeline Albright from 1997 to 2001. Man, we have come a long way!

In the business world, more and more women and people of color are "climbing the ladder" into powerful leadership positions that until just recently were reserved for mostly white males. Ursula Burns, an African American woman, was recently appointed President of Fortune 500 company Xerox Corporation with the expectation that she will move up to CEO when current CEO Anne Mulcahy steps down.

I recently returned back home to the northeast to attend the funeral of my father-in-law and while there, took the opportunity to visit the church that my family called home for 14 years. What a gift it was to meet and talk with their newly appointed senior pastor. She was a woman with a gentle and loving spirit and from what I could tell, a very dedicated and strong spiritual leader. There are still many religions and denominations within those religions that do not recognize woman as equal to men, especially when it comes to spiritual leadership but I'm positive the day is coming soon when this archaic and somewhat juvenile belief will be a thing of the past.

If you are a regular reader of the One Planet United, you know that what excites me most is when the evidence continues to pile up that the collective consciousness of humanity is continuing to unfold in a positive direction. It is an exciting time to be alive and witness the many evolutionary changes that are unfolding such as the equality of all people. Let's all help do what ever we can to keep it going.

"You Must Be Dreaming"

This past week I had to make a trip to my local post office to drop off some mail. Little did I know that a few brief words from the man that was servicing the window that I stepped up to would be the inspiration for this week's column. I needed to check the weight on some oversized envelopes which contained One Planet United information that I was mailing to some people across the country. The worker behind the counter told me that I needed an additional nine cents of postage on each envelope so as he printed the extra stamps and began to stick them on each envelope he would apply a stamp and say the word "dreamer." As he would apply the next stamp he would again repeat the word "dreamer." I realized that as he was applying each stamp, he was looking at the name on the return address label that said One Planet United. I asked him if his comment was related to the label and he said yes. He said it was a nice thought but that I was dreaming if I thought our planet could become united.

I told him that to some, it is not in their consciousness that this could be possible but to others it is only a matter of evolving to a higher consciousness that the possibility and probability will occur. We can't really know when, but if we look back in history and in our way of thinking about things, it is really encouraging to know that change can occur.

To touch on just a few areas, let's look back a little more than five hundred years ago when all those living believed that the world was flat. Some fellow comes along and figures out that they've been unaware all along that the world is round. Go back one hundred and fifty years ago to see that to own an African American as your personal property was not only OK, but people used the Holy Scriptures to justify it being acceptable. Fifty years ago, "people of color" as blacks were called back then could not use the same public toilets as whites. When I was in high school back in the early seventies, you were definitely in the "cool" crowd if you smoked cigarettes. Through education, time and a "higher consciousness" a large number of teens now look at smoking as stupid and extremely "uncool."

There are countless other examples of what we thought a generation or two ago were normal and acceptable. In many ways we came to a place of "higher consciousness" in our thinking and realized that we were quite "unconscious" at the time. That's where my belief comes in that we can one day become One Planet United. Call me a dreamer, but all change for the better begins with a single thought and then follows with the belief that it is possible. There is an example of this called "The 100th Monkey." It was a scientific study on animal behavior done by a group of scientists back in the 1950's. The end result of these studies was that when enough monkeys were taught a new behavior, the rest of the tribe began to follow suit. Incredibly, they found, monkeys that were even on different continents began to change their behaviors as well without being directly taught. The conclusion was that when a certain critical number achieves new awareness, it is then communicated from mind to mind, thus bringing a whole new consciousness.

If you can fast forward one hundred years from now, it is quite interesting to think about what the people alive at that time will think about those issues today that seem to be troubling our world. Differences in Religious and spiritual beliefs, war and political infighting, gay issues and same sex marriage, and how we take care of the disadvantaged in our society. I believe that as our consciousness continues to evolve and be raised to higher levels as it has in most every area of our awareness and thinking that it is very possible to believe our world can become united. It starts with each individual person seeing their neighbors as spiritual beings that we are to love, respect and care for. As individual people begin to become conscious of the fact that we are all in this together, there is hope that transformation can take place. It won't happen today or tomorrow, but it can over time if more and more of us continue to envision a world where the souls and hearts of all people become united as one body. A famous quote from the late Mohandas Gandhi states: "You must be the change you want to see." Let's continue to evolve to that higher place.

"Don't Move the Fence, Knock It Down"

Today's column will ask us to look at all the ways we separate ourselves from those who are different from us in any way and challenge us to do what we can to become bridge builders among everyone we meet. The idea came to me through a profound story that I read a while back that spoke to me very deeply and challenged me to see where I put up fences in my life that divide me from my fellow human beings.

The story goes like this. In the Second World War, a group of soldiers was fighting in the rural countryside of France. During an intense battle, one of the American soldiers was killed. His comrades did not want to leave his body on the battlefield and decided to give him a Christian burial. They remembered a church a few miles behind the front lines whose grounds included a small cemetery surrounded by a white fence. After receiving permission to take their friend's body to the cemetery, they set out for the church arriving just before sunset.

A Pastor, his bent-over back and frail body betraying his many years, responded to their knocking. His face, deeply wrinkled and tan, was the home of two fierce eyes that flashed with wisdom, passion and grace.

"Our friend was killed in battle," they blurted out, "and we wanted to give him a church burial."

Apparently the pastor understood what they were asking, although he spoke in very broken English. "I'm sorry," he said, "but we can bury only those of the same faith here."

Weary after many months of war, the soldiers simply turned and walked away. "But," the old pastor called after them, "you can bury him outside the fence."

Cynical and exhausted, the soldiers dug a grave and buried their friend just outside the white fence. They finished after nightfall.

The next morning the entire unit was ordered to move on, and the group raced back to the little church for one final goodbye to their friend. When they arrived, they couldn't find the gravesite. Tired and confused, they knocked on the door of the church. They asked the old pastor if he knew where they had buried their friend. "It was dark last night and we were exhausted. We must have been disoriented."

A smile flashed across the old pastor's face. "After you left last night, I was saying my night prayers and I began to feel very troubled and full of shame. I could not sleep, so I went outside early this morning and *I moved the fence.*"

From this story we can ask ourselves, "Where do we have fences built to keep those who are not *our kind* out?" Of course most of these fences are not physical structures but fences in our minds and our hearts. We have built them over the years, some built for us when we were children, which keep us believing that somehow we are different and perhaps better than so many other people. This is the type of thinking that One Planet United is trying to change because it is in this form of divisive thinking that so many of our chances for unity with our fellow brothers and sisters become lost.

The story of the pastor and the soldiers asks us to move the fence so that we can begin to include people of other kinds (religious beliefs, skin color, sexual orientation, financial status, political views etc.) One Planet United says let's take it even further. Instead of moving the fence, let's knock it down.

"What Are You Laughing At?"

Is it true that some things are funny and some are not? When people tell jokes or stories, should a line be drawn as to where we stop when it comes to humor? One Planet United has addressed this issue in the past, but feels it is time to revisit the topic and try to continue to bring awareness to the idea that what we laugh at speaks loudly for who we really are, as a society and as individuals.

I was up late one night last week and decided to watch Jay Leno, the host of The Tonight Show, only to check out his beginning "monologue" and hear what the topic of his jokes were. I'll tune in every six months or so, to see if much has changed regarding what he uses for his material. Sadly, not much has changed and the audience was still laughing. The entire piece was about ten minutes in length and here are the five topics/people he told jokes about. Michael Jackson (being charged with sexually abusing children), James Brown (charged with beating his wife while drunk), Kobe Bryant (being charged with rape), Martha Stewart (allegations of stock fraud) and the war in Iraq. Is it just me or is it true that none of the above topics are funny?

The thing that makes this situation so troubling is that Jay Leno whips through his monologue with what seems to be no awareness that the topics of all his banter are all about the misfortune and tragedy in these people's lives. What makes it worse is that the audience helps it along. I wonder if he would be able to joke about the Iraq war if he had a child that was fighting on the front lines, or if his wife had been raped by a celebrity. Is it possible that some people in the audience have had a child sexually molested and only appear to be laughing? What about the man who might be watching from his cell block who is in prison for beating his wife in a drunken rage? Does he ever think that every one of these people that he is making fun of is a human being with feelings? Does he realize that every one of the people he jokes about have parents, siblings and relatives that have to live through the tragedy with their loved one?

Today's column is in no way a personal assault on Jay Leno. There are countless other talk show hosts, both on television and radio i.e.: David Letterman, Howard Stern and many others, who have become multi-millionaires joking about people and topics that when we look close, are not funny at all. In fact, it was reported just this past week that Jay Leno is Hollywood's latest billionaire! Let's ask ourselves, how did people like this become rich and famous? The answer is, because we laugh. Because we laugh, we are validating their act and encouraging them to continue.

The respect and dignity of all human beings is at stake if we laugh and make fun of others tragedy and misfortune. People are always going to fall short and make mistakes. It is part of the human condition. What the hope of today's column is, is that people become more aware of ways we can lift up those who have fallen and not be a part of our society that tears them down. Also, to encourage you to tune out the people whose livelihood is achieved by joking about the tragedies of others. If we don't tune in, they have no audience. And if they have no audience, they might then realize that it is time to change either their material or their career.

"See First the Soul"

We live in a world today where division among people seems to be the norm. Whether it is by financial status or skin color, political beliefs or religious affiliation to name a few, all people seem to fall into a few categories which often time separate themselves from their fellow human beings. They either feel less than or better than those who are different than they are, which is what One Planet United believes is at the core of most of the strife and unrest that is present in today's society.

In the Bible, Jesus often spoke of becoming like little children if you are to find the kingdom. Unfortunately, we all one day grow up and become adults and that childhood way of relating to others seems to fade. We can learn a powerful lesson if we can become as little children when it comes to accepting and loving all people. Children do not separate themselves into groups and it is my belief that this happens because they "See first the soul." Children do not look at others and wonder how much money they have, or what religious faith their family practices. They don't see skin color or what kind of designer clothes you might be wearing. Children only look at the soul of another, which is where differences do not live. They are what One Planet United calls an S.T.D. In OPU language, an S.T.D. is a "Stranger to Division."

What is the human soul and how do you define it? That is quite difficult because it is something that can't be seen. According to scientific studies, the human soul weighs about the same as a feather. It was found that at the moment of death, a persons weight lessens by only 22 grams. With that information, could the human soul be that important? It is such a small part of us, but is it really? Is a little tiny chip important to a computer or is fuel important to a 5 ton vehicle? Can we actually see things like electricity or air? We can't see them with our human eyes, but we all know of their powerful effects on our lives.

I believe that most of us don't see the souls of another because like conditioning our physical bodies through exercise and discipline, the same is necessary to develop a connection with the soul. Through prayer, meditation and other ways, you first must develop that connection with your own soul and when you do, you can then see the soul of another. Children naturally live from their souls but as they grow up are often taught to disconnect from their souls and to see all the differences in others in a negative way.

If we can develop our souls to see the soul of another, so much could change in our society. If you first saw the soul of your children, could you possibly harm them in any way? Could you retaliate with someone who has just cut you off in traffic or treated you indifferently in a checkout line? If you first saw the soul of another, could you possibly feel superior to them for any reason? Could you tell a joke or laugh at a joke that is at the expense of someone else's tragedy or misfortune? If people first saw the soul of another, could there be shootings, domestic violence, gang fights, and war?

The hope of One Planet United is that more and more people will take the time each day to do whatever it takes to develop a connection with their own soul, thus recreating the way we all relate to one another. The hope is that one day, we all can become S.T.D's and that will only become possible if we "See First the Soul," first in ourselves and then our neighbors.

I Remain an Optimist

I'm a little crazy, right? You might say being optimistic that all people will one day live in peace and harmony with one another is pretty pie in the sky thinking. For me, I'm choosing to remain optimistic because I continue to see signs that divisive thinking, feelings of superiority and "group think" are slowly giving way to a sense that we are all one as the family of humanity.

I witnessed two more examples this past week in the media that gave me reason for my optimism. The ABC news magazine show 20/20 devoted an entire one hour program to the study of human prejudice and the built in tendencies that all people have to stereotype people that we either don't know, don't like or don't understand. It was a study which showed that the best way to heal these built in attitudes is to first realize that we have them (self knowledge.) And of course by airing this program in primetime, it challenged the viewer to do an inventory of their own thinking and the ways that they relate to people who are different than they are. The most moving part of the program was the story of former white supremacist and skinhead Tim Zowell, who served time in prison for beating up Jews and homosexuals. This same man who lived day to day hating people who were not "his kind" was now working as an employee at the Tolerance Museum in Los Angeles, California. Today, Tim spends a significant amount of time speaking to large audiences about the harmful effects of all hate and prejudice, regardless of what form it takes.

Secondly, I read in a recent Newsweek article (Aug 14, 2006) an in depth interview with Dr. Billy Graham, the most well known conservative Christian evangelist on the planet. He has spent more than six decades preaching his view of the Christian faith to millions around the world. The interview was quite interesting though because Billy states that he has changed as he has gotten older regarding his conservative views toward people of other faiths, Islam included. Where he once believed and preached an exclusive theology, he now says that he believes differently and that he no longer takes a stance regarding any superior claims of his faith. He says he has a much more connected feeling to all people and that his rigid views of salvation have changed. When asked whether he believed heaven would be closed to good Jews, Muslims, Buddhists, Hindus, or secular people, Billy answered, "Those are decisions that only God can make. It would be foolish for me to speculate on who will be there and who won't ... I believe the love of God is absolute. God said he gave his son for the whole world, and I think he loves everybody regardless of what label they have." This is a very different view than he once had where he adamantly claimed that only Christians would see God in the hereafter. Later in the interview, Dr. Graham was asked if he believed the religion of Islam was what some evangelists, his own son Franklin Graham included, termed a religion of "evil and wickedness." Billy replied, "I would not say Islam is wicked and evil. I have lots of friends who are Islamic. There are many wonderful people among them. I have a great love for them."

These positive and affirming comments coming from such an important figure in the religious world keep me optimistic that our consciousness as a people is continuing to grow in a positive direction. We're not there yet but evolution takes time. Just know that as we continue to grow and evolve as a people, we can surely remain optimistic that a united planet is closer at hand than ever before.

Peace is a Verb

A few weeks ago, I was fortunate to have been invited to attend an interfaith prayer vigil for peace that was being held in North Miami. The vigil was in response to the death and destruction in South Lebanon and Northern Israel. It was a gathering of community religious leaders from many different faiths as well as leaders and advocates for religious, social and racial equality. Senator Bob Graham delivered a message from a political view on the history of the Middle East and his observations as to why the killing continues.

There were five different speeches given by the chosen speakers but one caught my ear more than the rest. This presenter's topic was titled, "Peace is a verb." He was challenging all who were in attendance to not just hope for peace or to just pray for peace, but to actually become activists that create peace. He said that peace is a verb and that we must "do peace." His talk was fully aligned with the mission of One Planet United which is to inspire people to take an active roll in promoting peace by embracing diversity, promoting unity and creating community.

Some would say, "What can I do?" or "I'm not really qualified to do anything that could change the consciousness of the world." Please read on if you were thinking of opting out. What can you do? Here are just a few suggestions that you can try that are action orientated to creating peace.

Take time to volunteer in your community. Say hello to everyone you come in contact with and greet them with a smile. Invite a neighbor for dinner. Write a 'letter to the editor" when you experience prejudice, hatred or division of any kind. Speak out against someone who tells a joke or passes along an email that is offensive to a particular group or minority. All of these require effort and demand that you "take action" but none would be too difficult.

Making peace a verb and putting this practice into action becomes somewhat more difficult in certain situations. Situations like broken relationships resulting from family disagreements or messy divorces. To "take action" and be a part of healing is not easy in this situation but it is necessary if we are to heal as a global family. In my own family there are broken and estranged relationships that will "take action" on their part to create peace. It is my hope that they will reach out to one another and bring healing to their relationships.

What about you? What "action" are you currently taking that is helping to bring peace and harmony to your relationships and your community. In your community, don't wait for someone else to do it. In your relationships, don't wait for the other person to initiate it. I'm following up the speaker's challenge that I heard at the prayer vigil to say, "Make peace a verb, make peace an action word." Start now. Start today. Become an activist and make peace a verb!

A Whole New World

This past week someone sent me a short quote that is the inspiration for today's column. As I have mentioned in the past, readers of the One Planet United column often share quotes, insights and personal stories with me that relate to the vision of a world in which unity, equality, respect and understanding of one another is the norm. I always read them and follow that by returning a message of thanks for their sharing. I also encourage the sender to keep helping to raise the consciousness of our society. Then, every once in a while, one comes along that I read, then reread and then copy it so I can read it again. I would like to share one of those that I recently received that fits this category. It is my hope that you too will read it, read it again and then copy it so you can read it again and again. Maybe you'll be inspired as well to pass it along to others so that this message can touch the lives of many others.

The quote comes from a prophet of the Baha'i faith. If you are not familiar with the Baha'i faith, it is a Religion that began back in the mid nineteenth century and today has over five million followers from every nation in the world. The essential teaching in the Baha'i faith is unity. Included in their teachings is the oneness of all religion, the equality of all races, the elimination of all forms of prejudice and the harmony of science and religion. The mantra of the founder of the Baha'i faith was, "The earth is but one country, and mankind it's citizens." The writing that was sent to me truly could be the creed for the One Planet United organization. I invite you to read these words slowly and adopt them as your vision of a new world. In the words of the Baha'i prophet;

"My hope is that through the zeal and ardour of the pure of heart, the darkness of hatred and difference will be entirely abolished and the light of love and unity shall shine; this world shall become a new world; things material shall become the mirror of the divine; human hearts shall meet and embrace each other; the whole world become as man's native country and the different races be counted as one race."

Imagine for a moment what the world would look like if we could all embrace these words and adopt them as our own personal mantra. It might look quite different from the world as we now know it. Why not pass this along to your family and friends as well as make a copy for yourself and leave it in a place where you can reflect on its meaning each and everyday. My belief is that if these words are embraced by enough people, the collective consciousness of society will have a greater chance to rise to a new level where all persons live in unity, harmony and community with one another and that divisions of race, religion, politics, nations, genders and others cease to exist. A whole new world if you will.

It's all in the Lines

In a recent article describing the space shuttle *Discovery*'s return to earth, it was noted how amazed the astronauts were at how beautiful the planet earth looked from a distance. They said that no matter what part of the globe they were looking at, it looked very peaceful everywhere. "We just flew over the middle east and I have to tell you, from up here it looks peaceful and quiet just like the rest of the planet," astronaut Piers Sellers told ABC News. "I think all of us are mindful from flying around and around this one little earth, that it's all we have. This is humanity's home and hopefully, one day we'll all get along."

Seems pretty simple when you hear it from this man's perspective. I have always been amazed when I see a photo of the earth taken from outer space how incredibly beautiful it is as well as the fact that there are no lines or borders separating states, countries or nations. Unfortunately, these man made lines and borders seem to be a large part of much of the trouble we are currently experiencing in the world. The border lines between Mexico and the U.S. are creating a significant amount of unrest, violence and division. On the other side of the planet, the death and destruction that is happening between Israel and Lebanon all begins at the "border" line that separates the two countries.

I was talking about this topic with my wife a few days ago. She told me that when she was a young girl, she shared a bedroom with her older sister. They had an imaginary line or border that went down the middle of the room. She went on to say that the only time they had any trouble was when one sister would cross the border on to the other side of the room. If they stayed on their own side, trouble was kept to a minimum.

In the future, I envision a world without borders. I believe this will come to pass when we reach a collective consciousness that this adolescent form of thinking and behavior is responsible for much of the pain and suffering we are currently seeing each and every day throughout the world. It is my belief as we evolve and mature as a people, we will see that these borders and lines are what keep much of the destruction, violence and deep division alive and well among nations, countries and people in general. It will be at this time that a new peace will come upon humanity.

The call from One Planet United is for humanity to wake up to adolescent and outdated modes of thinking and behavior such as I describe. We will hopefully one day see that borders and lines, which in reality don't even exist, must become invisible if we are to live in harmony with all people. As the astronauts attested to, from a distance, there are no borders. I wait in hope for this realization to be embraced by all nations, all countries, all states and oh yes; all siblings as well.

Collective Consciousness for Peace

It is known that when enough people reach a collective consciousness no matter what the issue, something happens. Sometimes the result is good such as when more and more people began to see that owning a human being as personal property was inhumane, slavery was abolished. In other times, when groups of people all become aligned with the same collective consciousness, it can be a bad thing. An example of that might be a youth gang in a local city who is bent on destroying a rival gang. No matter what the issue, a group of people thinking with a collective consciousness usually means something is going to happen or something will change.

Here are a few things that have changed for the better that I believe are directly related to a collective consciousness waking us up to see things differently.

Smoking: It is now illegal in most cases in the United States to smoke in a public building or establishment. Think back to 30 or 40 years ago. You could be at an appointment to see your doctor and there would be ashtrays on the tables in the waiting room. It was perfectly normal to be allowed to smoke in an airplane, although you had to sit in the rear of the plane. Believe it or not, the teachers that I had while attending a catholic boy's school in the 1960's smoked cigarettes while they were teaching us the day's lesson.

Drinking and Driving: I'm not proud to admit it, but 35 years ago when I was in high school, the driver behind the wheel of most cars driven by teenagers was no more sober than the other occupants in the car. The term "designated driver" did not exist. Although teenage drinking is pretty much the same as it was when I was a kid, there is a good chance that the collective consciousness of young people has changed so that the possibility of having a sober driver in a car full of teenagers is a regular occurrence.

Equality of Women: Less than 100 years ago, women were seen as an inferior gender and were not allowed to cast their vote in public elections. Now it seems likely that we might have a woman running for president in 2008. Have we evolved in our thinking?

These examples are just a few of many. We continue to evolve as human beings and are continuing year after year, decade after decade, to raise our collective consciousness and see things in a different light. What I want to bring to light in today's column is a call for a collective consciousness for peace.

Peace first within ourselves, then with our neighbors and finally with all people everywhere.

To reach this goal, I believe that we first must begin to see every person that we come in contact with as our equal. Not better than or less than. We can achieve this by what I call "See First the Soul." That means that before you see anything in another that can create any division see first that they have a heart and a soul within them. What we often do today in our current consciousness when looking at another person is, we size them up and base our findings on the "group" they happened to be aligned with. We ask, "Are they our kind? Are they good looking? Did they go to a college that I feel is the right college? Do they have money? Are they popular? Are they a particular race that I don't have issues with? Do they worship the same God as me? Did they vote for the right presidential candidate?"

All of this kind of thinking keeps us from looking at each individual as a person who has a heart and a soul. Thus it increases the difficulty to reach a collective consciousness for peace among all people. It's a challenge, but haven't we reached a new and better consciousness in many other areas of our thinking and relating? Let's start today to do all we can to reach this collective consciousness by first finding peace in our own souls which ultimately will turn into all of us being at peace with one another. Sounds pretty awesome, doesn't it?

The End of Better

I'm better than you. She's better than her. They're better than us. What's up with better? Is their a more important thought in the way we divide ourselves as people than the word better? If you live in an upscale neighborhood, do you feel you are better than those who live on the other side of town? If you wear designer jeans, does that make you feel better than someone who is wearing Levi's? How about cars? If you drive a "status car" and you pull up to a light next to someone in a Buick, do you somehow feel a little better? What about race or religion? If you are white do you sometimes feel you are better than someone who is black? Or maybe if you are black, do you feel better than someone who is white? Christian-Jew, Jew-Christian? Here's a big one. What about financial status? If you are well off financially, do you often feel superior to those who are not? And one more for old time's sake. You graduated from a top University and your neighbor graduated from Community College. Do you feel that somehow, you are a little bit better? Young-old, tall-short, fat-thin, the list goes on and on.

What about this word better? Where did it come from and how did it filter into our society? The dictionary says the word means more useful, suitable, or desirable than another or others. I feel this definition doesn't do any harm when you might be using it to describe the fit of a new dress where one fits *better* than another, or as a student you happen to be *better* at Math than English. Where it does great harm is when we use it to make ourselves feel superior or better than another person, group or organization. It is a disease that has grabbed the hearts and thinking of many people in our world and in turn has created a lot of hatred, bigotry and prejudice which exists in our society today.

One Planet United is all about uncovering where we (humanity) divide ourselves from one another, so it is time we make the shift from thinking or believing we are any better than anyone else for *any* reason at all. We all showed up on this planet in a diaper and we're all leaving in a shroud, so how different or better can we really be from one another. It's time to put an end to better.

All Up In Smoke

When you think about how we as human beings divide ourselves against one another, today's topic would not be the first that comes to mind. Our first thought might be prejudice against someone with a different skin color or maybe someone with a sexual orientation that we don't agree with. After that, you might think of someone who has different political beliefs from your own or maybe someone who worships God by a different name from the God you worship.

Today, One Planet United is addressing a very strong area in which we divide ourselves against one another and that is people who smoke and people who don't smoke. Now in the grand scheme of things, this can seem to be a bit trivial, but underlying the surface, it is a big deal. There are so many negatives from both sides as in where smokers want to be left alone, while non smokers want to be sure that they don't have to be around to breathe second hand smoke. It has become a National problem and both sides don't feel like they are getting enough respect.

On the job, or in the home, there are deep resentments from both sides. When an employee has to slip out the back door every hour to answer a craving and have a smoke, the employer is wondering if they should deduct one hour of pay each day for smoke breaks. Meanwhile the employee would say if they were allowed to smoke at their desk, they wouldn't have the need to take it outside and use company time. It's the same inside the home. The smoker will need to exit on a regular basis to feed their craving, while the family is inside feeling resentful that a cigarette is more important than they are.

It's an issue in offices, homes, restaurants, airports and anywhere else that smokers cross the paths of non-smokers. What we need to realize though, is that this issue will most likely never go away. The way to better deal with it from both sides is to put yourself in the other person's shoes. Become aware of how the person on the other side feels.

If you are a non smoker, understand that most people who smoke want to quit or have tried many times and failed. Understand that addiction to nicotine is as powerful as addiction to alcohol or drugs. Nicotine *is* a drug. Also, accept the fact that some people who do smoke enjoy it and have no intention of quitting. If you do smoke, be aware that those who complain about it are not just trying to be annoying to you. Breathing second hand smoke is extremely unpleasant and unhealthy. One day I was at the beach with a family member who was smoking a cigar and a lady who was at least 25 yards away came over and asked if he would put it out. She said that she was breathing the smoke and that it was very distasteful. He put it out but at the same time, he had a resentment at her and thought she was being very intolerant. Unfortunately, he didn't realize that even though we were outdoors at the beach, the smoke was still overpowering and offensive.

In closing, OPU would like to suggest a new way to any smokers who have tried desperately to quit, and have been unsuccessful. It is a way that you can save two lives at the same time. Decide how much money you spend per week on smoking. If you smoke a pack of cigarettes each day and the cost is approximately $3.00 per day, the total is approximately $21.00 per week or $84.00 per month. Each day, put the money away and at the end of the month, write a check for $84.00 and send it to a local charity.

By trying this way of kicking the habit, not only will you be adding years to your own life, you'll be taking the money that used to go for cigarettes and know that it is now going to help save or enrich the life of another. By thinking of doing something good for others while at the same time, doing something good for yourself, it could be the way to finally kick the habit. I wish you success.

An Alternative Escape

Today's column is to inform you of an alternative escape. To the movies that is. A few years back when you would be sitting in a theater waiting for a movie to begin, an intro would often come on the screen inviting you to "Escape to the Movies." I agree that when I am watching a movie for two hours or so, I am definitely escaping any issues that are present in my everyday life.

The problem these days though is that it is getting harder and harder to find a movie that I want to escape to. Often, my wife and I will look through the week-end movie listings in the newspaper to see if any new motion pictures have been released that we would want to see. Unfortunately, most often we take a pass. At other times, we get the desire to go to our neighborhood video store in search of a movie we might have missed that we wanted to see. There too, we often leave empty handed after cruising the hundreds of movies that are on display.

It could be age or just that I see the world a lot differently than years past, but when it comes to movies, I'm most often looking to be inspired, challenged or enlightened. Someone asked me one day not long ago what my three favorite movies were of all time. As I thought about it, my thoughts went to films that not only inspired me but showed me the strength of the human spirit and the beauty of love in human beings. I said "Forrest Gump", "The Color Purple" and "A Beautiful Mind." Films such as these have a similar theme which usually has a positive effect on the audience, often inspiring them to be better human beings and to see the good in all people.

Whenever I have the chance to see a great film that challenges me, inspires me or lifts my spirits, I find myself wondering why someone in the movie business doesn't make more movies that can bring such a positive impact to the screen. I think media, television, movies and radio are the key vehicles that can bring powerful messages to masses of people.

So here's where the alternative escape to the movies comes in. A small group of writers, movie producers and directors have formed an organization called The Spiritual Cinema Circle and their mission is to create films that are an alternative to the main content that Hollywood is producing. They have pooled their talents, finances and resources and are hoping to inspire many to use the experience of going to the movies as one that can raise the consciousness of our society to what is good in people and how the human spirit has the power to heal and overcome large obstacles.

They have begun a "Movie Club" that you can join which is quite similar to a music or book club. You sign up and pay a monthly fee and you receive

2 to 3 movies each month that are all created with uplifting and value based themes. Also they have come up with the idea to begin to show the movies they are creating to collective audiences in a unique way. Convinced that no large movie production company would take on the distribution rights of their films, of course for fear of lack of profits, this group is distributing them on their own. Their idea is if they can get enough people to embrace their type of films, than Hollywood might get the message that millions of people are looking for alternatives for movie entertainment. Thus, the ultimate goal is to change the course of modern day movie entertainment as it is known today, and the negative effects that many believe it has on society.

Here is how they have set up the distribution of their films. When they are ready for distribution, they have individuals set up a place to view the film, either at a movie theater, a house of worship, or a hotel banquet room. The unique approach to this is that they designate one day only to view the film, so anyone who wishes to see it will all be viewing it on the same day. These films are shown in thousands of locations all on the same day so it has the opportunity to have a large impact.

So, if you are one who likes to escape to the movies, why not try an alternative escape. You'll be challenged, inspired and enlightened while at the same time helping raise the consciousness of *all* people.

Note: To learn more about "The Spiritual Cinema" go to www.spiritualcinemacircle.com

Some Say it's a Choice

In today's column I want to address a very intense issue that continues to be a hot button topic for many people. I'm talking about the issue of homosexuality and the two main differences in beliefs that people have. That being, is it a choice to be gay or is a person born gay? Unfortunately it is most often debated today in religious circles regarding topics, most notably, gay marriage. But underneath all of the debate, there is still a profound difference of how individuals side with the issue that continues to perpetuate great division.

You might wonder why this topic would be addressed in the One Planet United column. If you think of all of the issues that divide people, some examples being religious beliefs, political views, pro war or anti-war and the like, the issue of individual's beliefs toward homosexuality are one of the big dividers of people at this time in history. The idea of the OPU column is to try to continually bring to light the areas where human beings seem to be most divided and try to offer insights or solutions for healing.

A poll was taken in 2004 in the L.A. Times which stated that 7 out of 10 people said that knew someone who is gay. I can't say that I know for sure, but I would venture to guess that if you asked the same people whether they think that it is a choice or that they were born that way, the same 7 out of 10 would say that they believe they were born gay. On the other hand, (I have no facts to back this up, just a hunch) if you asked the 3 out of 10 who don't know someone who is gay if it's a choice, I believe they would say it is a choice and that they could become heterosexual if they wanted to.

Depending on where you stand, consider some of the following facts. If you ask someone who is gay when was the first time they knew something was different about their sexuality, the majority will tell you that they knew they were different somewhere between the ages of 6 and 12. Also consider that at our time currently in history, many experts in the medical field will state that the number one cause behind suicide and attempted suicide of young people ranging in age from 15–24 is the inability to live with the shame felt by the knowledge that they are homosexual. Consider that probably the most ridiculed and joked about minority today is the gay population. Just recently I have been in conversations with two different people where the topic of homosexuality came up. The first man's comment to me was "Well, I don't have a problem with fags." Another fellow who I had asked what his church believed regarding homosexuality said in these exact words, "We don't allow faggots and homos in our church." Would a person choose to be a part of a group that is continually being referred to in such derogatory terms?

My own personal beliefs on this subject come from the fact that I have come to know many gay people and for the most part, they are no different than the straight people I know other than their sexual orientation. To go a bit deeper though, my feelings come from not only knowing people who are gay, but getting to know them in a way where they trust you enough to share what it is truly like to live as a gay person in today's society.

A very close gay friend of mine shared with me one time while openly crying, how much he has hated himself all of his life because of his sexual orientation. He said he has had to deal with self hatred all of his life and has had to battle with the difficulties of living in a world where you are looked at by many as a freak or a despicable human being. He shared with me that he had one time attempted suicide and continues to this day to see it as an option to stop his life of inner torment. After sharing with this man and becoming a friend that he could trust to share with, I say today that it would be the strangest thing if he was choosing this path where fear, ridicule and self hatred are his daily companions.

It is my belief that the healing of this division between these two different views will only come when those that see it as a choice have an opportunity to truly get to know someone who is gay. Ask them to honestly share what it is like to live in a society that often rejects, ridicules and makes fun of them. They might then come to a new understanding, compassion and a whole new perspective toward a group of people that often deal with an inner struggle and sense of shame on a daily basis. There is an old saying that always keeps me trying to put myself in another persons shoes before I make a judgment about how I feel toward them. It is called "Contempt prior to investigation." I ask anyone that before they make any judgments regarding this divisive issue, be sure that you've investigated what it is really like to be gay in today's world. If we harbor ill feelings toward a group of people that we know nothing about, we're only practicing one more form of prejudice and intolerance which are the attitudes that keeps us from being a more united people

"Give Em' The Finger"

Here's the scenario. You're driving down the road trying to make your way as best you can through the maze of traffic that confronts you each day. You happen to slow down too fast or speed up too slow or do something else that annoys another driver in your path. As they speed by, you notice that they are not at all happy with your driving skills and the way they convey that message is through a gesture that you can't possibly misunderstand. That gesture would be the extension of their middle finger aimed skyward in your direction accompanied often by a look of disgust. If you are a daily driver, you have surely been greeted in this manner. I find it interesting that one little gesture can pack such a powerful message. Not a word is spoken, but everyone knows what is being said in a non verbal way.

I was thinking of all the other non verbal gestures we often use each day to send a message to other people. Here's a few; the shaking of hands or bowing in respect as a form of greeting; a wave of your hand to let another driver go ahead of you; a "thumbs up" signal to convey approval; the two finger sign for peace; the two handed symbol for "time out"; the athlete pointing to the sky after scoring a touchdown, a winning basket or hitting a homerun. Hopefully you've never met up with someone who was running their index finger across their neck while at the same time looking in your direction.

I want to use today's column to try to kick start a new non verbal gesture that has unlimited potential for good in the world. It's called the One Planet United sign for peace. Let's begin today by giving people the finger. That's right, "Give Em' The Finger." There is only one difference though. We move over one finger to our index finger. Whereas a gesture using your middle finger sends a message of disgust, disapproval and anger toward a fellow human being, the gesture of using your index finger could be such a powerful tool for approval, oneness, unity, forgiveness and brotherhood. What would it be like if you happen to accidentally cut someone off in traffic and as they went by you, they gave you the "index" finger as a sign saying, "Hey no problem, I've cut people off myself. I'm a lot like you."

What would it be like if this gesture of oneness became a normal way of greeting anyone you come in contact with no matter what the situation? It has the potential to change the way we look at and relate to all people. It is a sign of honor and respect and a way of saying "We're all in this together" and that we are all members of one and the same family. The family of humanity.

You might be saying this is a little silly, a bit of a stretch or impossible to have people embrace. Someone sometime long ago was the first person to use their middle finger as well as shake someone else's hand to express a particular message. Why not be a part of starting a new gesture that has incredible potential to bring about unity among all people of the world.

I think of the growth of this new idea in the same way literally millions of people now support and embrace the courage of Lance Armstrong and his battle with cancer. What started as one yellow "Live Strong" wristband on one person's wrist turned into hundreds then thousands and now millions. It has become a powerful message of unity amongst millions of people all over the world.

So let's get it going. Start it today. Whenever you get the chance, regardless of the situation, "Give Em' The Finger." The One Planet United finger. Make it known to others, no matter if it's in a positive or negative situation, that you honor and respect them as fellow human beings and that your wish for them is one of unity, oneness and brotherhood.

"Who Are These *People*?"

Jessica Simpson and Nick Lachey, Kenny "Babyface" Edmonds, Tom Cruise and Katie Holmes, Sharon Stone and Kate Moss, Beyonce', Jay-Z, Renee Zellwegger, Jennifer Lopez, Antonio Banderas, and Marc Anthony. "Who are these people"?

They happen to be the people featured on page four of the local newspaper one day last week. Each day in the front section of the paper, there is a half page with the heading titled; PEOPLE. The list above represents this particular days featured people and what is happening in their lives. Here's the lowdown.

Jessica and Nick deny they are splitting up. "Babyface" confirmed that he is in fact splitting up with his wife Tracey although they will remain best friends. Tom and Katie are "expecting. Sharon is standing by the side of Kate who is in trouble with her modeling career due to her love for cocaine. Beyonce has embraced the name "Sasha" as her new stage name and is also remaining hush-hush regarding her relationship with Jay-Z. Renee is starring in a new horror movie. J-Lo was on the set of her new movie co-starring Antonio Banderas accompanied by her husband Marc Anthony. Are these the PEOPLE that we as a culture want updates on?

This same day a few hours later, I was in my local grocery store and there it was again. I was waiting in line at the checkout and I was surrounded by ten different magazines and newspapers focused on celebrity updates. Here were the cover stories featured in the week's PEOPLE Magazine. The secrets of Desperate Housewives, Brad Pitt's divorce and the troubles in the life of Prince William.

So once again, I ask, "Who Are These People" and why do they take up so much of the headlines? A couple of other questions I would ask. Why the title "PEOPLE"? Shouldn't these articles, feature stories and magazine titles be called "Celebrity Update"? Also, do you ever wonder why this information sells so well and why millions of us have an obsession with the lives of movie stars and celebrities of all kinds?

First, I feel that by giving the title PEOPLE to these stories, it legitimizes that the lives of these people are very important to us in some way. Secondly, if we are fascinated with the lives of celebrities, it seems likely that our children will learn to be also. Could it be why so many young people' role models and hero's today are named Brittany, Diddy and Paris?

I bring this topic to light today because I hope to create a certain awareness and change in consciousness. First, that we wake up as adults and realize that being infatuated with the lives of Hollywood celebrities is quite meaningless, and second that we begin to teach our children about the lives of people who have made an impact on the world, thus creating role models that can inspire us all.

I recently came across a book titled; "Architects of Peace" by Michael Callopy which is a book of short stories that features seventy-five different men and women who have lived their lives focused on being advocates to help change our world for the better. These are stories about humanitarians, spiritual leaders, politicians, scientists, artists, and activists of all kinds with names like Elie Wiesel, Jane Goodall, Mother Theresa, Thich Nhat Hanh, Dr. Maya Angelou, Maya Lin, Nelson Mandela, Corretta Scott King and many more.

I can't help but think how awesome it would be if more coffee tables in the world had books like "Architects of Peace" on them rather than a copy of the most recent issue of PEOPLE magazine. I say if we are going to spend our time reading about the lives of people, let's focus on those who have lived their lives to lift up mankind and make our world a better place. What these particular people have been led to do could also be the inspiration for all of us to reach a higher consciousness and be transformers of the world ourselves.

Note: Copies of "Architects of Peace" are available for purchase on the One Planet United website. Visit www.opunited.org and click on OPU Store.

Tis' the Season of Peace

In the next couple of weeks, millions of us will be celebrating this special season in an assortment of ways. We will be buying gifts for our loved ones, decorating our houses with lights, attending parties, and preparing mountains of food to share with those closest to us. It is also a time where many take the saying, "good will toward men," seriously. For many, it is a holy time and a happy time. For others, it is a painful time, brought on by memories of loved ones who have passed away or raw recollections of family holidays that went wrong.

However you choose to celebrate this holiday season, let us all remember that the essence of this season is peace. Let us all hold this as our highest thought amidst all the hustle and bustle of all that we "must get done."

My inspiration for today's column comes from a poem that asks us all to focus on one thing; to focus on being a person of peace. The author of the poem is Mattie J.T. Stepanek, whose life ended prematurely at the young age of twelve. He was a poet, a public speaker, and advocate for many causes, but those who knew him best called him a peacemaker.

I've always been in awe of the term "peacemaker" when it comes to describing a human being. When I think of the word "peacemaker," I think of people like Maya Angelou, Desmond Tutu, Dr. Martin Luther King and President Jimmy Carter. Of course these are the people who have accomplished great things and have gained universal recognition because of it. But think about all the people who live their lives as peacemakers that we have never heard of by name.

What I'd like to suggest today is that we all take on the title of "peacemaker" What would it be like if all people made a conscious decision above all else, to be a person that is devoted to bringing peace to all situations? Maybe we think that this is a title only reserved for people who are famous or who have written books on the subject. I believe that every person alive has the ability to be a peacemaker, be it in their home, their school, or in their community. If this becomes our focus, most of us won't become famous, but we will be a part of building a united planet, where peace is known above all things.

So let us focus during this season of peace on becoming a "peacemaker." Think about the transformation that would take place if upon awakening each morning, we all look inside ourselves and say "Today, my priority above all else, will be to bring peace to every person and situation I encounter today." Of course, because we are human, we will often fall short of the goal, but when we succeed, the whole world will benefit.

I'll close today's column with a prayer. It is the prayer inside a poem written by Mattie Stepanek. Let us all observe and try our best to carry out his wish for peace.

December Prayer
No matter who you are, say a prayer this season.
No matter what your faith, say a prayer this season.
No matter how you celebrate, say a prayer this season.
There are so many ways to celebrate life.
No matter who, no matter what, no matter how you pray,
Let's say a prayer this season,
Together, for peace.

Wishing you a season of hope, joy, happiness, and most of all, a season of peace!

Note: Copies of Mattie J.T. Stepanek's book of poems, "Journey Through Heartsongs," are available on the One Planet United website. Visit www.opunited.org and click on OPU Store. 100% of all purchases help support the ongoing work of One Planet United.

The Disease of Elitism

When you think of or hear the word elitist, you probably think that it only pertains to issues regarding class status. A person who thinks that his or her class status is superior to all others is usually referred to as an elitist. But what about those people who believe their religion is better or somehow more real than another? Or how about when it comes to politics? It's pretty intense when you hear someone from one side of the aisle talking about the inferiority of one who is on the other side. One definition in the dictionary defines an elitist as one who believes they are the "cream" or the choice part.

I refer to this type of thinking as a disease because it is like an emotional cancer that is rooted in many individual's hearts. I liken it to cancer because it is extremely destructive, especially if it goes unchallenged. On an extreme level, this kind of thinking and way of perceiving the world can be seen and heard in an assortment of ways. The thing that makes this such a terrible force against people loving one another and living in a unified world is that most often, it goes unchallenged. Most often, people who live and think in elitist terms don't even know that they are spreading this disease. The fact that they believe they are superior to another in any regard, perpetuates all of the things that keep human beings from truly being allies with one another.

The big question is, how do we uncover where this kind of thinking is present and how do we get folks to wake up to the harm that is being done? A good place to start would be to stand up to someone when you hear them talking with an elitist or supremist attitude. Tell them that they are squashing the integrity of another human when they speak out in the belief that somehow their class, race, religion, political view, sexual orientation etc. is somehow superior to another. I say, speak out and confront this form of intolerance, prejudice and bigotry. It takes a little courage, but I see it as one way to help heal this mode of thinking. It is always been known that if you do not speak up when someone is saying something you whole heartily disagree with, you imply by your silence that you agree.

I encourage you to take a risk, be brave and help be a healing agent against all forms of elitism and attitudes of supremacy. Speak out and speak out often when you hear it. For today, you and I can be a strong force to help heal the deadly disease of elitism that has infected so many.

Handguns; Myth or Reality?

Tell me if you see something wrong with these headlines that all appeared on the same page of the daily Fort Lauderdale newspaper I read a few mornings ago. Take a deep breath. Here goes; "1-Year old boy killed, man hurt in shooting"—"Couple, quadriplegic son, 20, shot to death"—"Gunfire cuts short teens future"—"5 die in church shooting spree." I was thinking that if I turned to the next page, I might have found more of the same. I began to feel a little sick and extremely upset so I didn't go on.

After seeing these headlines, I found myself feeling baffled, angered, puzzled, dazed and wondering what is going wrong, knowing that these are pretty much normal headlines in newspapers all across the country. I found myself asking, "What is in the minds of people who wake up in the morning and by the time the day has passed, they have pulled a gun on someone and snuffed out a life." Is it just random evil that is a part of life? Somehow I just can't go along with that theory.

I often write about the need for the consciousness of all people to reach a higher place if we are to ever know peace on earth. Normally, I'm referring to such social diseases such as prejudice, intolerance and group division. To heal these harmful situations, it takes time, discussion, and increased awareness and understanding. On the other hand, when it comes to murder or the taking of a human life, we don't have time to talk. Too many people are being killed everyday and it just doesn't make sense. Something has to be done.

I want to say that there is a place we can start and that is to eliminate the 65 million handguns that are currently in the U.S. Let's start with this question. Are you one who believes that owning a handgun for self defense is a good thing? Studies show that this thinking is a myth. Who do you know that owns a handgun and has used it in self defense? I wonder what the percentages are of the times where a handgun is a helpful thing versus a harmful thing. From what statistics say, it seems to lean seriously toward the negative and always at much too high a price. That being, the taking of a human life. Let's return to the one of the headlines.

"Gunfire cuts short teen's future." This story is about one teenager dissing another on how much cooler his car was than the boy he eventually shot and killed a short while later. How does the story end? Did the two boys have an argument that ended in a fist fight and a bloody nose? Not exactly. Somehow, an angered 17 year old boy left and returned to the scene with a handgun. He shot and killed the other boy in cold blood.

One public health researcher was quoted saying, "People without guns *injure* people. People with guns *kill* them."

The sad thing is that this story and ones like it are in the headlines each and every day and they all involve someone using a handgun to deal with their rage, anger or discontent. Do we really need handguns on this planet? Am I missing something as to their positive effects on anything or anybody? Let me tell you something. Just writing this column today has made me extremely angry and frustrated, but since I don't own a gun, I'm going to have to deal with my anger in another way.

What a concept. No handguns in the hands of anyone. Do you think the murder rate in this country would drop? Maybe the headlines would look more like this. "5 hurt in church punching spree"—"Couple, quadriplegic son, 20, kicked by angry man"—"1 year old boy unharmed in yelling drive by." I know some people believe that there is something good about being able to own a gun. I say to those who do, scan the headlines for the next week and get back to me and let me know your findings.

Note: To learn more about the studies, staggering statistics and myths of the self-defense handgun, visit www.banhandgunsnow.org or The Violence Policy Center at www.vpc.org. There is also a book available written by Josh Sugarmann titled "Every Handgun is Aimed at you." Josh is the executive director of The Violence Policy Center.

"Hey Man, that Ain't Funny"

Do the jokes we laugh at tell us a lot about who we are as people and as a society? Are some jokes appropriate and some not or is it that if it is funny, than anything goes? What kind of jokes do you laugh at and what do you consider funny? I believe that the jokes we tell and the one's we laugh at tell us a lot about how we see the world, especially other people.

I first became aware of this a few years ago when the O.J. Simpson murder trial was in the papers and on the TV every day. Although this was an extremely tragic event, it seemed to grip the world in a way I found void of compassion for all of the pain and heartache that many people involved had to endure and still do to this day. What to me was the most painful thing I saw in all this was that many found humor in this story. I would hear people in my place of business telling the latest O.J. joke they had heard. The newspapers would have cartoons dedicated to making fun of the ongoing trial. The late night talk show host's would spend most of their allotted time for their monologue telling jokes about O.J. and the saddest part of this was that their would be three to four hundred people in the studio audience that would laugh and applaud after each joke.

Should we be joking about and laughing at other people's tragedy and misfortune? I believe we need to wake up and see how damaging this is and how it keeps us from what we need more in our world than anything, which is compassion for others. It is hard to have compassion and empathy for others if you can also be one who tells jokes or laughs at jokes about other people's pain.

Was O.J.'s story just about O.J. or did his children's mother die a tragic death and they must spend the rest of their live's without their mom? Did Ron Goldman's parents lose a son in a horrific way and now have to deal with this pain forever? What about Nicole Simpson's family? Her parents and her siblings and all the extended family will have years of heartache to deal with. If we look at the reality of this story, can their be anything funny about it, and should we be a part of either telling or listening to a joke about it? When we tell a joke about Bill Clinton and the Monica Lewinsky saga, are we thinking of the shame and embarrassment that his daughter Chelsea is dealing with? Is the situation that has come forth in the Catholic Church something that should be joked about? Think of the pain that the abused and their families have to deal with. I tuned into the late night talk shows last week just to investigate what the topics were in their monologues and found that the majority of the jokes that were being told by the host and laughed at by the audience were about Saddam Hussein. How can we joke about that? Lives tragically altered and changed for countless people by war and the terrible rule of a sick dictator. What about jokes about gays, or jokes about people of a different nationality than you? The list goes on and on.

Let's look at it another way. If we personalize it, would it still be funny? If it was your son that was killed in Iraq, could we partake in a joke about Saddam? If you found out that your Dad was molested 30 years ago, would you laugh at a joke about priests molesting children in the Catholic Church? All of these tragedies that people laugh and joke about involve real people with hearts and souls that have been badly broken.

OPU asks you to take a risk the next time someone begins to tell you an inappropriate joke or you receive one in an email. Let them know that you would rather not hear it. Tell them that what they are passing along to you is something that you personally don't find funny. It takes a bit of courage to cut someone off who begins to tell you an inappropriate joke, but if more of us would begin to do this, we would begin to see that these type of jokes might stop. You would then be a person who is helping honor and respect *all* people, instead of helping to tear apart their dignity.

"Did you hear the one about" …? Hey man, if you think about it, that ain't funny.

A Creed for All

I often receive emails from OPU column readers that give me the inspiration to write a new column based on the thoughts or comments they have shared. Recently, I received an email from a regular reader who said he wanted to pass along something that was meaningful to him that he thought was aligned with my column. He said "These 65 words have helped shape my life as I try to serve as a living example of them." He was referring to the Jaycees Creed.

After reading it, I was inspired to share it in the OPU column because it speaks so closely to what I write about each week. It also reminded me that about a year ago, another reader sent in a creed that inspired me to write a column called "The Four Way Test" which is the creed of the International Rotary that is recited by all of their members at the beginning of every meeting.

The Jaycees Creed states:

We Believe:
> *That faith in God gives meaning and purpose to human life*
> *That the brotherhood of man transcends the sovereignty of nations*
> *That economic justice can best be won by free men through free enterprise*
> *That government should be of laws rather than of men*
> *That earth's great treasure lies in human personality and*
> *That service to humanity is the best work of life.*

If you think about it, not all creeds are a good thing because many times they are written with an "us and them" mentality. They are often designed to divide. But I'm realizing more and more that some creeds are good and could be adopted by all of society. What would the world be like if the Jaycees Creed was adopted by us all? Every individual? Every state? Every Nation?

The line that jumps out at me the most is "That the brotherhood of man transcends the sovereignty of nations." This is the creed of One Planet United and speaks loudly to the place humanity must reach in its thinking if we are to become a society of peace and unity. Imagine what the world would look like if this was a reality. War cannot exist if all of society is one brotherhood. Nor can violence, crime, prejudice or division. If a societal brotherhood exists, there will be fellowship. Where fellowship exists, there will be mutual respect, honor and the promotion of equality.

Is the world a brotherhood today? Not quite, but as in all evolution, things take time. It must begin inside the human heart one person at a time. We first need to take our own inventory and see if we are aligned with any group or thinking that keeps us from being a part of the brotherhood of man. Next we need to take action in helping this evolution process along by finding ways to help build bridges and foster unity with all people whether it's in our own communities or across the globe. It is really up to each and every individual to be a part of this change in helping the whole world to become a brotherhood. If we all adopt the Jaycees Creed, the brotherhood of all of humanity will be that much closer to being a reality.

CHAPTER 8

Community

A Bunch of Ones

Are you someone who wishes to see changes in the world but often find your-self thinking, "What can I do—I'm only one person?" Are you frustrated about situations or events that happen every day and wish you could do something to help change it? The war in Iraq, children going to sleep hungry, animals being euthanized due to overpopulation, the everglades continuing to shrink? Are these some of the situations that you have a yearning to help change but find yourself asking, "What can I do—I'm only one?"

I want to take this opportunity to let you know that you are not alone and that there is a movement now sweeping the world that you can be a part of. It is a movement born out of humanity's response to social injustice, religious division, political disease, and environmental irresponsibility. It is comprised of billion-dollar nonprofits to single-person dot.causes. These groups collectively comprise the largest movement on earth, a movement that has no name, leader, or location, and that has gone largely ignored by politicians and the media. Like nature itself, it is organizing from the bottom up, in every city, town, and culture and is emerging to be an extraordinary and creative expression of people's needs worldwide. So rest assured, you are not alone. There are a bunch of ones and a myriad of groups that are being born everyday helping our culture to continue to evolve.

As the co-founder of the non-profit organization One Planet United, there are times that I become discouraged, asking "Can our organization really make a difference when there is so much division among races, religions, classes, political groups and gender groups in the world today?" There are times when I have become quite discouraged and want to give up saying, "Maybe things will never change." It is times such as this that someone will always send me an email, a note or make a suggestion that brings me back to my original passion for being a dedicated worker for social change. This time it was a friend who sent me a link to a website that he knew would inspire me to know that I am not alone and that we all have to keep working for the change we want to see in the world.

The website that my friend was encouraging me to visit was about this movement of which I speak. It outlines the ten year study of a man named Paul Hawken who has uncovered over 130,000 groups, both small and large, who have devoted their lives to social, environmental and political change. He suggests that there are most likely thousands more. These groups are as close to you as your own town or city in which you live and expand all around the globe. When I went to this website and watched the short video of the study,

I was suddenly struck by the idea that I am *not* alone and that there are thousands of people working everyday to help heal the world.

So to you who say, "What can I do, I'm only one," I hope you will realize that you are not alone and that there are a bunch of ones around the globe who are taking action to help move our society in a positive direction. Take heart and know you are not alone. Come join the movement; you're help is greatly needed.

Note: You can learn more about Paul Hawken's book and his study by visiting www.blessedunrest.com Be sure to "Click on the video."

Blessed Unrest

In my previous column titled "A Bunch of Ones" I wrote about the amazing work of author Paul Hawken who did a ten year study that uncovered over 130,000 individuals and small groups who work to help our culture to continue to evolve for social justice, religious unity and environmental healing. He calls it a movement with no one leader, no dogma and no by-laws. He says that the movement comes out of a response from individuals and small groups who want to help the world to heal in many of the places that are hurting us all.

Many of these individuals and groups have been born out of what Paul Hawken calls "Blessed Unrest." A group or organization was started or an individual took action because something deep down was causing unrest in their souls. They acted because something was bothering them so much that they had to do something. They had to respond and get involved.

Those you would be familiar with that fall into this category would be people like Martin Luther King Jr., Rosa Parks and Mother Theresa. They all had such unrest about what they were seeing in the world that they said, "I must do something." At different levels, the 130,000 groups and individuals that Mr. Hawken uncovered were responding in the same way. They all had a deep down sense of unrest and decided to take action and join the movement.

In my own personal life, this is how One Planet United, the organization was born. It came out of my unrest for all of the division I saw among people in the world. I felt a calling to start an organization that would promote unity and understanding among ALL people. We are now three years old and our programs are having a profound effect on many.

So what bothers you? What gives you unrest about what is happening in your community or in the world as a whole? Does the fact that many children go to bed hungry bother you? How about women being victims of violence? Maybe you want to see the everglades preserved or fewer animals euthanized each year. What I'm advocating is that you find out what it is that bothers you and take action and get involved. Join the movement that was born out of humanity's response to social injustice, religious division, political disease and environmental irresponsibility.

If I had endless space to write in this column, I would point out countless examples of people who took their unrest and turned it into a blessing. Unlike a man I met a few weeks back that was so angry about the fact that there are more and more people living in the U.S. who do not speak English. My suggestion to him was to take his anger and instead of turning it inward and doing nothing about it, try to figure out some way that he could be part of the solution. I asked him to possibly consider becoming a tutor and begin teaching English in his spare time?

The latest "Blessed Unrest" story I heard was just this past week. It was the story of a young 15 year old girl named Dallas Jessup from Vancouver, Washington who was being honored by CNN as a "Local Hero." Upon learning about the staggering statistics of date rape and abductions of young girls, and that a recent national study declared that one out of four teen girls will be date raped or sexually assaulted, she decided to "take action." Dallas had recently achieved her black belt in Tae Kwon Do and decided to create a video that would be available to teach teen girls three moves that would render an attacker helpless thus giving the victim the needed time to escape. Dallas' passion to do something with her unrest is now a national program with corporate sponsors, doing a great work to save lives. To learn more about her program, and how you can download the free video to share with teen girls in your community, log onto www.justyellfire.com

So, is there something that bothers you that you would like to see changed? Do you have a sense of unrest about something that is important to you? Why not turn your unrest into a blessing for the planet? Join the "Blessed Unrest" movement and help be a part of a "Bunch of Ones" that is transforming our world, one person and one community at a time.

We *Must* Be Neighbors

With the Olympics just recently coming to a close, I'm thinking back to the opening ceremonies of a few weeks ago. It was One Planet United at least for an evening. Every minute or two, the athletes and representatives from different countries entered the arena waving their flag and joyously waving to the thousands in the stadium and millions watching on TV around the world. It was mentioned by the broadcast crew that there were just over 11, 000 athletes representing 202 different nations in which it took almost two hours until the final country was announced and welcomed. It was truly amazing to see certain nations in the world that I had never heard of. In the graphic underneath the name of the nation, would be a slide showing the total of what the population was. Some of these nations had over 1 million people living there and I was unaware that it even existed.

It began to strike me as overwhelming, as to how many people populate our world as a whole. We are approximately 6.2 billion people all sharing the planet we call earth. At that moment, a thought came into my mind. I began to think that if I share the planet with all these people, than we must be neighbors. Then I was asking myself, who is my neighbor really? Is it the person who lives next door or across the street? Maybe we're neighbors if we live in the same development or the same town.

The odd thing is that the further geographically we are from someone, it is usually less of a chance that we feel that we are neighbors. But is that really true? Think about it for a minute. Have you ever been away on vacation far from your home and met someone that lives in your town, county or state? Don't you automatically feel a bond as if you're neighbors? I experienced this a month ago while on a trip with my family to the mountains in North Georgia. A couple came up to us to pet our dog "Angel" and we struck up a conversation. To our surprise, these folks were from Plantation, which created an immediate bond, since we live in Coral Springs (Plantation is a town 10 miles south.) I thought for a moment, why is that? If these folks were from another place in the U.S, there most likely would have not been the same feeling.

It happened another time last summer when my wife and I were thousands of miles from home on a trip in Italy. We were in a very crowded area in Florence where thousands of people were gathered and I noticed a girl wearing a t-shirt from the same university that both of my children attend in Florida. I was so excited that I went up to her and said "We must be neighbors." The same experience often happens when you meet someone years later who grew up in the same town or went to the same high school as you did. Being connected is an automatic.

Now, I wonder how great it would be if it was an automatic that we felt connected to *all* people and not just those who share a geographical area in common with us. What would our society look like if we came to know that we are all part of the human family? What if we raised our vision to see that our neighbors are every person on the planet? Wouldn't peace among people have a greater chance to grow and multiply? The only reason we often feel unconnected with someone geographically is either a body of water or a border that was invented by human beings.

The best chance for peace in our society is for more and more people to come to the realization that in reality, we are all citizens of the same world. We have to come to the awareness that the word "must" in the phrase "We *must* be neighbors" is an action word. We can know that deep down we can say to anyone, "Hey, if you live on this planet, that means we must be neighbors?"

One Planet United believes that if we are to come closer to a peaceful world, coming to the realization that *all* people are truly our neighbors, is for sure, a *must*.

Just Hangin'

It's a very familiar sight on most days when I drive into my neighborhood at the end of the day making the last few turns before I pull into my driveway. Perhaps you have witnessed this scene as well. A group of kids, most often teens, are hanging out pretty much not doing much of anything, but for sure enjoying the camaraderie and closeness that their peer groups often thrive on. It reminds me of back when I was a young teenager and the times I was "just hangin" with my group. The feeling of being accepted was what gave my group its life and identity.

Today's column is directed to these groups of kids that can be found in neighborhoods from coast to coast. It comes from one of the eight programs designed by One Planet United called "We _Must_ Be Neighbors." This program outlines a number of ways that people who live in the same developments or neighborhoods can not only connect in a deeper way with those they live around but also shows ways to reach out to the community in general. Some of the ideas are directly aimed at inspiring kids and one in particular is called "Neighborhood Youth Outreach Project." It was designed with the kids in mind who are "just hangin" and as I said, not really doing much of anything. The idea is for the neighborhood group of kids to take on a community building project that they do together with their friends that they are always hanging out with. Thus, they still get to hang with them while at the same time be involved in a community outreach project.

Some projects include food drives, clothing drives, car washes and the like. The group can "adopt a house" of someone who is sick or elderly and help take care of weekly chores. Here's how it works.

The group of kids come together along with one or two parents who all live in the same neighborhood. The parents sometimes can help out where needed. Decide on a project and choose the charity, organization or individual that you want to do the project for. If it is a car wash, do it as a fundraiser and donate the money to a designated charity. If it is a clothing drive, find the places in your community that accept used clothing. If it is a food drive, locate the local food pantries in your community or possibly start one from scratch. If you decide on helping ("Adopt a House") a particular family or individual in your neighborhood, let them know of your intentions.

Next, make up a flyer that outlines that the youth of your neighborhood have taken on a project and that they are asking everyone to help. Describe in the flyer how your outreach project will work. If you are collecting food or clothing, make it known that you will be coming by their front door on a designated day and time and you will be happy to pick up their donation. If it is a car wash, note the day, time and location that you will be holding it. When the flyers are completed, place them at all the houses in your neighborhood.

I personally would be proud to live in a neighborhood where I knew that the youth that live around me are socially aware of people in need and have decided to take on an activist role in making a difference. I'd also be the first one at a car wash if it was right in my neighborhood. Normally, I pass right on by local car washes that kids are putting on because either I didn't know about it or when I did notice it, it was too late to stop.

Developing community builders and personal activists for positive social action among young people is where it's at if we want to see a more caring and compassionate world in the future. To the young people who I speak to today, I say go ahead and "keep hangin" but while you're at it, why not initiate an outreach project in your neighborhood and be a part of making your community and ultimately the world, a better place for all.

Note: You can access the "We Must Be Neighbors" program template from the One Planet United website. This program outlines many community building programs that anyone can initiate in their neighborhoods as well as provides samples of flyers.

Visit www.opunited.org

The Human Community

When you hear the word community, what is the first thing that comes to mind? Maybe it is the religious community you are a part of in the faith you practice. It could be a school or college you attend that has a very strong feeling of school spirit or student community.

There are those who align themselves with a political or economic community, although some who find themselves in certain economic communities would choose differently if they could. The recovering community is another powerful group who are people that have been freed through 12 step programs from the power of harmful addictive behaviors and thinking. There is a sense of community in the recovering community that is the actual power that helps human lives heal in many ways.

The reality of community is everywhere around us and is an expression of something deep within us all which is a need to connect with like minded people. It gives us a certain degree of security in the path that we choose to take and in the ways we choose to think. It gives us the sense that we are not alone, which is also something that is built in to the human psyche. We gain a sense of well being when we know we are connected in community with others.

There is a harmful side to community that we all have witnessed at one time or another. It can be when one street gang decides to try to take down their rivals. It can show up at a high school or college football game when the fans from one side start a fight with the fans from the other side. On a larger scale, isn't the U.S. a community that is in a war with another community? That being a terrorist community. Most often when you think of the word community, it is a positive picture of something good and positive. Unfortunately, groups of people that become aligned with others and join forces are not always joining their hearts for something good.

One Planet United believes that there is one community which to this day does not exist. It is community that could begin to heal the world if we would just embrace it. What community is this? It is called the Human Community. It is a community that would align one human being with another and create a sense of oneness and unity with *all* people. It would mean it wouldn't matter what neighborhood you live in, if you went to college or not, who you voted for or where you might choose to worship the God of your understanding. It would be the only community in existence that did not have a dimension of exclusion, either by design or circumstance.

The unfortunate thing is that The Human Community does not hold weekly meetings, send out a quarterly newsletter or hold annual fundraisers to remind us of the community we choose to align ourselves with. The only way you can embrace The Human Community for now is in your heart and your mind. You can join this community just by beginning to see *all* people as your brothers and sisters. Let's use this as our place to start. Come be a part of building a new and great community. The Human Community.

The Great Blackout

Once again, we were able to see the difference of people living and reacting from their hearts a few weeks ago during the great blackout in the northeast. When life took what seemed like a tragic turn for a day, men and women once again showed that when we reach a level of fear and uncertainty about life, we tend to leave the familiarity of living from our brains and intellect, and go to the deeper level of our hearts and souls. With a very similar look and feeling of the tragedy of Sept 11th, this day, August 14th 2003, asked us once again, do we really care about our fellow human beings that we share this planet with and do we really love our neighbor? From what I could see on a TV screen and read in a newspaper, it looked like the answer was yes. People were helping people escape subway tunnels and tall buildings, as well as giving rides to strangers. A friend of mine who lives in New York City shared with me on the phone that people had a sense of love and concern for one another while this whole event was unfolding, that was beautiful to witness. It could only be that people were acting from a place in their hearts.

When one person in the dark subway train was reaching out their hand to grab the hand of another, do you think the helping person worried what color skin the other person had or what political party they belonged to? When the driver of the car that was offering the stranger a ride out of a crowded and hot city, do you think he or she was concerned if their new passenger was gay or straight? How about the person that was helping another out of a stalled elevator to safety? Was there a question of this person's religious affiliation or financial status?

It seems at times such as these, all differences that we might have with others cease to exist and all that remains is that we are all one people, deeply concerned for one another. It's like we "blackout" our prejudices and our differences. There was a poem that found its way onto the internet following the dark day of Sept 11th that describes what most people feel deep down at the heart level, but often ignore, until we reach a time of tragedy. It is called:

"ONE"

As the soot and dirt and ash rained down, *we became one **color**.*
As we carried each other down the stairs of the burning building, *we became one **class**.*
As we lit candles in waiting and hope, *we became one **generation**.*
As the firefighters and police officers fought their way into the inferno, *we became one **gender**.*

As we fell to our knees for strength, *we became one* **faith.**
As we whispered or shouted words of encouragement, *we spoke one* **language.**
As we gave our blood in lines a mile long, *we became one* **body.**
As we mourned together the great loss, *we became one* **family.**
As we cried tears of grief and loss, *we became one* **soul.**
As we retell with pride of the sacrifice of heroes, *we become one* **people.**
WE ARE
One Color, One Class, One Generation, One Gender, One Faith, One Language,
One Body, One Family, One Soul, One People.
We are the power of One.

One Planet United encourages all of us to keep this attitude going at all times and not just in times of tragedy. Imagine what our world would be like if we embraced this attitude day after day, each and every day. If we can see and connect with the *heart* of another, our differences and prejudices are sure to melt away.

"Don't Just Stand There; Volunteer"—(Part 1)

Feeling down? Is your life one of endless periods of difficulty and negativity? Are you thinking that maybe you should run to your doctor and ask if he thinks a certain pill "might be right for you?" The way things are going; there are lots and lots of people running off to their doctor looking for a cure for their feelings of emptiness, isolation and desperation. Many people have bought into the advertising that says if you are not "feeling yourself" talk to your doctor and ask him if a certain drug might be right for you to feel good.

You've probably seen these advertisements yourself. Typically it will be a scene of a middle aged woman who looks extremely depressed and in a state of despair. Within the sixty second ad, she has taken a prescription from her doctor that is a magic pill for feeling blue and is now standing at an open window with the breeze blowing in her face, smiling and in a sate of peace and serenity. Well, I admit, advertising works for it is known that prescription medication is being dispensed by doctors at an all time high to supposedly cure the pains of depression.

When a person is feeling down or depressed, the most common reason is because they have become overwhelmed with all of the things that are not going right in there lives. It is often related to problems on the job or in marital relationships. As well, it can be in difficulties in raising children or the fact that you can't find a person to be in a relationship with. All of these conditions as well as many others can easily find a person in a lonely place and feeling isolated form the rest of the world. It is quite natural to feel down and empty when our lives have taken a turn into a place that involves disappointment, loss and an unknown future. The question is, is there a natural cure?

One Planet United would like to suggest an all natural, non prescription remedy that you might want to consider before running to your doctor for "the cure." It has been called by many in the health field as "all natural Prozac." The suggestion is to become a volunteer. It is known that if you begin to think of another person and reach out to help them, your own problems automatically lessen. There is a natural drug that is released inside our body which comes from leaving ourselves and our problems aside for a time and giving our energy to someone else who has a need for help. Whatever might be ailing you often disappears when you are actively involved as a volunteer in another person's life or in a cause that you believe in. It is a natural way to feel good about yourself and your life because you are reaching out to help another.

If this idea speaks to you, there are opportunities everywhere around you. Local schools, nursing homes, homes for unwed mothers and troubled youth, and countless other places are all in need of volunteer help. There are over six hundred non-profit organizations in Broward County alone that cannot survive without volunteers. These non-profit organizations are set up to serve the public interest and those who are in need of help and their volunteers are what keeps them strong and making a difference.

What are some of the areas that these organizations are making a difference? Suicide prevention, feeding and clothing the homeless, combating social prejudice and intolerance, helping those affected by addiction, domestic abuse, child neglect, those with mental and physical handicaps, the elderly, the terminally ill and the list goes on. By reaching out and offering to volunteer to get involved and help, you will not only be helping those in need but you will be helping yourself as well, the natural way. By giving your time and energy to others, you'll likely see that what was ailing you has either disappeared or greatly lessened. Try it and see if this kind of cure doesn't work naturally. Find out if becoming a volunteer "is right for you."

Note: For volunteer opportunities in your community, log on to www.1-800volunteer.org
This organization provides direct connection throughout the U.S. to local volunteer opportunities that match interests, skills, and the common desire to make a difference.

"Don't Just Stand There; Volunteer"—(Part 2)

Today's column is part two of some thoughts and insights on the benefits to all who become involved in volunteering. I believe strongly in giving back to people who are less fortunate or to causes that are doing good things in the community. I believe as well that it is one of the most important things we can teach our children. If children are taught from an early age that giving is more important than receiving, we will be raising a generation of kids that will look at the world in a way that can benefit our society as a whole.

I wanted to take this opportunity to share my experience as a parent and some of the ways my wife and I taught our kids the importance of giving as well as volunteering. We were members of a church for many years back home in the northeast that provided numerous ways to get involved in helping others, so our kids got to be a part of many different ways of volunteering. We fed the homeless in New York City, helped out at holiday time in shelters, rebuilt abandon buildings in the South Bronx, and once provided housing for a ten year old girl from Brooklyn who's Mom was in prison and didn't know who her Dad was. As well, our kids were present and sometimes part of the decision making process when we provided financial help to people and organizations that we chose to support.

One thing I found out as they got older and began to enter their teenage years was that it wasn't quite as easy to get their attention when it came to discussing their involvement and importance of helping others. As teens often do, they enter the world of self centeredness and reaching out to others isn't exactly on the top ten of their priority list. We still felt it was important to encourage them, even though at this stage of their lives, they were much more reluctant to participate in any volunteer activities.

It is at this time as a parent, once in a while when they resist most, you have to become creative. Some would say that when a parent stoops to the level of bribery to get their child to participate in a volunteer project that they are guilty of bad behavior. Well then, I have to admit, I'm guilty. It was back in the mid 90's and my son was not happy at all that we uprooted his life and moved to Florida from the Northeast. He was struggling with his new surroundings and was avoiding not only getting involved in worthy causes, he wasn't even trying to make new friends. An opportunity at our new church was being offered to high school kids to go away and attend what was known as "Work Camp." This is a program where four to five hundred teenagers from many parts of the country travel all over the U.S. to rebuild and repair houses in poor and needy neighborhoods. I wanted him to attend this program for two different reasons.

One was that the possibility would present itself that he could get to know some new friends. I also believed strongly that a week focused on rebuilding houses and spending time helping people from extremely poor areas in the country could be a life changing experience for him.

Here's where the bribery part comes in. He had been talking about how much he wanted to purchase a set of fancy rims for his car, but was having a hard time putting up his own money to purchase them. I told him I had a deal he might not be able to refuse. I told him that if he would attend this week long work camp program, which up this point he was totally resisting, I would pay for the rims for his car. It only took him a few seconds to think about it. It turned out to be a deal he couldn't refuse because he agreed to go.

It turns out the trip was such a positive experience in his life, that he voluntarily attended the next two summers without any push or bribery tactics from my wife or myself. That was eight years ago and he is now a twenty four year old adult who lives on his own in Atlanta. I have to say that although I am very proud of his achievements in his personal and business life so far, I'm most proud of the fact that last year he volunteered to coach a youth basketball team, and just recently began mentoring a young fatherless boy.

We must always teach our children the importance of reaching out to help others and it is best of course if it starts when they are young. Of course it benefit's those on the receiving side, but it equally benefit's the one on the giving end. It builds good traits like character, integrity, and selflessness but more importantly, it builds a better world for everyone.

"What's in a Name?"

While standing at the checkout, I smiled at the girl who was working the register and said "Good morning Sonia!" She said good morning back to me but was a little stunned that I greeted her by name. It's probably most peoples impression that employees who work in retail are asked to wear name tags so if a customer has any problems, they can report them to management. I use it as an opportunity to greet someone who often times is going through the motions of their job with little interaction with customers.

As Sonia and I continued our discussion, I noticed the woman who was just finished checking out in front of me. She seemed eager to know why Sonia and I we were having such a friendly exchange. I greeted her as well and said, "Good morning, I wish you were wearing a name tag like Sonia because then I would feel like my greeting was personal." She exchanged a greeting in return while at the same time, Sonia decided to show me the woman's name on her membership card. I once again greeted the woman in front of me, but it was personal this time. I said, "Good morning again Debra. It is nice to see you today." It was pretty cool to now see three total strangers connecting with one another all because we used our names.

For this brief moment in time, the three of us became more than strangers that might possibly exchange a friendly nod. By using our names, we all became real people. I said to them that we might have just discovered the answer to peace and harmony in the world. They both were wondering where I was going with this thought. I said, imagine what it would be like if every person on the planet wore a name tag. It would mean that every person would now become a person when in a public place. Conversations among strangers would then become common place.

I did not know it, but this interaction between former strangers was to continue. As I was pulling out of the parking lot and passing "my new friend" I lowered my window and said, "Goodbye Deborah, have a great day." I was going slowly enough that she walked toward my car and said, "I think I know you from somewhere." As we exchanged the possibilities of how we might have known each other, I found out she was the mother of a girl who I had worked with on an interfaith concert sponsored by One Planet United last year. As I drove away, my spirits were soaring. I had to believe that my two new friends' spirits were soaring as well.

Could it be that if we all started wearing name tags, we would cease being strangers to one another? Could wearing a name tag make every person we come in contact with all of a sudden become a real person rather than just a blur that some of us see as we go through our day to day routine? If you ask "What's in a name?" I would have to say a greater chance for unity, harmony and fellowship with all people.

CHAPTER 9

4 Steps To Promote Unity

Get Closer

In the next eight weeks I will be sharing the insights of what One Planet United has titled: The Four Steps to Promoting Unity. Many people say that they desire to live in a world that is less divided and where the idea of loving your neighbor is not just a dream but a reality. The Four Steps to Promoting Unity offer concrete ways that all of us can initiate to help create a more peaceful and united society.

The Four Steps to Promoting Unity are; Get Closer, Educate Yourself, Speak Up and Take Action. Today's column will address the first Step; Get Closer.

It seems to be part of our deeper nature that when we are afraid of something we will usually retreat. We will quickly turn and run when brought face to face with something that we are afraid of. What first might come to mind would be a fierce animal or an enraged person with or without a weapon in their hand. If we found ourselves in this type of scenario, we would normally run as fast as we could. But what about things we are afraid of that do not pose any threat of danger? What about our deep seated fears of particular groups of people? Isn't our reaction the same? Whether it is a homeless man on the street, a bunch of youth dressed in the current day "gangsta" attire or a motorcycle gang coming down the street, isn't our ingrained reaction to turn and go in the opposite direction? Could this not also include a religious group that we don't align our faith beliefs with or a political group from "the other side of the aisle?" When it comes to prejudice and intolerance, this is normally where we tend to go. We tend to go further away with no interest in getting to know "them."

I believe that the opposite must happen if we are to begin to heal the many forms of prejudice in our society. We must go against what our inner nature tells us—run away—and adopt the position to "Get Closer." We have to adopt the same attitude of a man that faced danger as a career named Steve Irwin. Steve was known as "The Crocodile Hunter" who unfortunately lost his life this past year doing the thing he loved to do best. Steve made the phrase "Get Closer" possible by showing us that his fear never kept him from getting closer to animals that would normally make one run as fast as possible in the other direction. His mantra while coming face to face with a scary looking "croc" was always the same; "He looks like he's going to bite. Let's get closer."

The idea of "getting closer" when it comes to prejudice, stereotyping, profiling, and intolerance is the way that understanding others will become more and more a reality. The people and the groups that we are most prejudice against are often those we don't know anything about.

Religious intolerance is most often fueled by a fear of getting closer to a person from a different faith. I have a friend who has sent me emails that show the plight of extreme Muslims and asks me if I still believe that Islam is a religion of peace. My answer back is that I truly believe that Islam is a religion of peace, but that it has been hijacked by political extremists who call themselves Muslims. I have continued to encourage him to "get closer" to people of the Islamic faith so he can learn more about what they believe and how they really feel about their faith.

In my own life, I have had the opportunity to get to know (Get Closer) many Muslim people and attend many conferences that discuss the true beliefs of Islam and I find them all to be loving people who desire peace as much as anyone. I just recently attended a conference called "Muslims in America" which I found fascinating and very educational. The Imam (spiritual leader) who was one of the speakers on the panel quoted scripture versus from the Koran that vehemently spoke out against the taking of any human life. One verse said that if a man takes even one life he is killing all of society.

Most of us who live with deep prejudice toward people of other faiths, political alliances, sexual orientations, nationalities, etc., do not really know those that that we are distancing ourselves from. If you ask someone who is prejudice toward homosexuals and lesbians if they have ever taken the time to "get closer" and get to know someone who is gay, their answer is more than likely going to be no.

In the next OPU column, I will share insights on the Second Step to Promoting Unity which is "Educate Yourself." Until then, remember that a sure way to dissolve much of the fear and prejudice in your own life is to "get closer."

Educate Yourself

In today's column, I want to describe step two of the "4 Steps to Promote Unity" called "Educate Yourself." The 4 Steps to Promote Unity come from the new book One Planet United and were originally developed for the new Diversity and Personal Activism (DAPA) training workshops for corporations, civic groups and teens now being offered by One Planet United. In part one, I talked about the first step in promoting unity which is "Get Closer."

How much of our own prejudice that lives both consciously and unconsciously inside our minds and hearts comes from lack of knowledge? How much of our fear of those who are "not like us" is based on ignorance and a lack of understanding? I'm not sure if there is any way to get hard facts and statistics as to what percentage fall into these two categories, but it is sure to be the reason for most peoples prejudice and intolerance.

This fear that lives deep within many people is exactly what keeps us away from learning about those who are different than we are. The idea of "getting closer" and "educating yourself" about people of different cultures, nationalities, religions, sexual orientations etc. does not sit well with most people, thus we remain a very divided people.

Educating ourselves offers the opportunity to remove the veil of ignorance and come out into the sunlight of being at peace with all people. Taking the time to learn about people who are different by any design is the hope of one day living in a united society.

If you are already resisting the idea, I challenge you to take a risk and see if your heart might begin to open by stepping out of your comfort zone and taking a leap of faith to educate yourself. Here are a few ideas to help you get started.

Visit a different house of Worship—If you are someone who attends religious services on a regular basis, chances are you will not find yourself mixing with people from different faith communities. By visiting a different house of worship, your whole understanding about people of different faiths will change. It is quite ironic that people who live together in the same community will purchase their groceries at the same food store, root for their children at the same soccer field, and call the same police department or fire department when help is needed, but when it comes to the practice of religious faith, stay very far apart. Why not go to a synagogue or mosque if you are Christian or go to a mosque if you are Jewish or Christian or a synagogue if you are Christian or Muslim. Look in your local paper and see if you see a notification of a religious speaker who will be talking about their faith tradition which is different than yours.

Visit your local library—Take out a book, a DVD or CD on any topic related to a group or culture that you are not familiar with such as the struggles of Martin Luther King Jr. and the difficulties of equality among races or the history of each of the world religions and the commonalities that they all share. Find a resource that describes what it is truly like to live as a gay person in today's society. There are a multitude of learning opportunities provided at local libraries.

Attend a multi-cultural or religious event—I just recently attended a 3 hour conference that was held at the local library in my community that was titled: "Muslims in America" It was fascinating learning so much that I did not know about the religion of Islam. I met with Islamic men, women and children who were outspoken about their love of life and their denunciation of terrorism in any form. I was fascinated to learn that women who wear a head covering *choose* to do so in response to their faith expression. It has nothing to do with being subservient and suppressed or dominated by men.

Many other topics can be found that can increase your understanding of groups or people that you don't know much about. Education is not only important for children to become successful adults, but is crucial for adults as well to be able to realize that the groups and people you might tend to stay away from are people who desire most of the same things in life that you do.

Cultural festivals, seminars, workshops and more offer great opportunities to educate yourself about people you don't know much about. Take the time to learn and you will see that your heart will let go of much of the fear that has kept you from truly experiencing the goodness that is within us all.

Speak Up

Today' column is the third in my four part series that is focusing on "The Four Steps to Promote Unity." The Four Steps to Promote Unity were developed by One Planet United as part of a diversity training program for corporations, civic groups and teens. The first step is to "Get Closer" and the second step is to "Educate Yourself." The focus of today's column is the third step to promoting unity which is to "Speak Up."

Speaking up when we witness prejudice, inappropriate humor and any other situation that demeans another person is not an easy thing to do for most people. It often feels safer to just go about our business and keep our opinions to ourselves. By "Speaking up" when we see these types of behaviors, we risk standing out and being called a "goody goody" or we might be told, "come on, lighten up." We might be looked upon as being a killjoy who people now feel have to be on guard when they are around us, for fear that the "moral police" will speak up.

Not speaking up in more serious matters has been shown to sometimes end in death or serious injury. Battered women, abused children, drunk drivers. We often witness serious situations in these matters and look the other way saying "It's really none of my business."

In less serious matters, there is still a feeling inside most of us that we should just stuff our feelings because by speaking up, it's sure to cause conflict and conflict is something most people will avoid at all costs. Instead of speaking up to a waiter and telling him that the steak you ordered medium was served rare, most of us will eat it anyway. If we are told by a doctor that we need a certain procedure done, we would never think twice to speak up to the doctor and ask what it is for. Questioning a doctor is one of the all time greatest fears that people have because a doctor represents "authority" and fear of authority runs deep in most all people.

Why is it that most people would rather remain silent than speak up when they see a situation that should or could be confronted? It seems that speaking up is risky because if you speak up and state your opposition to a situation that is happening, there is the chance that conflict or rejection will surely follow.

When it comes to healing the prejudice and intolerance that lives in many people's hearts, it is imperative that we have the courage to speak up and let people know that their actions or comments are degrading, offensive or belittling. By remaining silent, we only help perpetuate the belief that offensive speech or behavior is OK. When we speak up, the offender will get a message that what they are saying or doing is wrong, thus presenting the possibility that they will change.

Many people of history actually lost their lives by opposing violence, oppression and prejudice. Dr. Martin Luther King Jr., Mohandas Gandhi, Dietrich Bonhoeffer, and Jesus were all killed because they chose to "speak up." Speaking up will, in most cases, not endanger our lives, but it does entail the possibility of retaliation, rejection or conflict. There is risk in speaking up, but by renaming silent, words and behaviors that help perpetuate hatred, bigotry, and prejudice will continue to grow under the surface.

It is my hope that when an opportunity to speak up regarding prejudice, intolerance or bigotry presents itself that you will take a risk and be heard. If more and more people step out of their comfort zone and speak up when it is called for, healing of our world will become a place where human dignity is held up high for all of us to celebrate.

In the next OPU column, I will share insights on the Fourth Step to Promoting Unity which is to "Take Action." Until then, remember that a sure way to help heal much of the prejudice, intolerance and ignorance that exists in the world today is to "Speak Up." Don't stay silent. The dignity of humanity is at stake.

Take Action

Today's column concludes my 4 part series on "The Four Steps to Promote Unity." The Four Steps to Promote Unity were developed for One Planet United's diversity training program called DAPA (Diversity and Personal Activism) for corporations, civic and faculty groups and teen groups. The first step is "Get Closer." The second step is "Educate Yourself." The third step is "Speak up" and the focus of today is the fourth step in promoting unity. It is called "Take Action."

For a majority of us, taking action is the hardest part but for sure is the most gratifying part of helping to promote the concept of community building. "Getting Closer" to those we are afraid of or don't understand is a must if we are to reach a higher consciousness and build community. "Educating Ourselves" is vital if we are to learn more about people who are different than we are. "Speaking Up" is crucial if we are going to begin to try to teach others the importance of protecting human dignity and creating a deeper understanding of the sacredness of all people.

"Taking Action" is where the most effective changes will take place. When individuals and small groups take up arms and begin to implement community building ideas and programs in the communities where they live, unity among all people will not be too far behind.

Many of us sit and wait figuring that someone else will do it. Many rely on the hope that if we elect the right person to office in the nation's capital or in our own towns and cities for that matter, that the world will turn around for the better. This mode of thinking is a fantasy and is unrealistic. A united society and a world in where all people honor and respect one another cannot unfold unless people begin to take personal responsibility and become active in connecting with those around them. It goes along with the old saying that says, "If you want a beautiful garden, you must pick up the hoe."

It is my hope that you will see the importance of taking action to build community and strive to connect with the hearts of those around you. We are very much a divided people but by taking action, we can all play a part in building a more united society.

Want some help in getting started? Visit the One Planet United website (www.opunited.org) and click on "Programs." Next, scroll down to "Community Building Programs." Here you will find many different ideas that you can initiate in your own community. These programs can be downloaded free of charge and require no money, education or training to implement. All that is needed is a desire to help embrace diversity, promote unity and create community.

Epilogue

It is my hope that the insights I have shared in this book have made you think and challenged you to take a closer look at the way you see and relate to your fellow man and woman and the world at large. Often times, the prejudice that we carry in our minds and hearts never gets challenged, sometimes because we are not even aware that it exists. Most of the people that I come in contact with that have deep prejudice for certain groups of people or certain individuals have never been challenged or encouraged to take a deeper look, thus making it difficult to heal.

All of us need to take a closer look at the way we see and relate to people that are different than we are. Let us come to a higher consciousness and begin to see that all people are essentially good and are worthy of honor and respect. Let us come to see what we have in common rather than where we might be different. Let us see that we all smile when we are happy and cry when we are sad, we all bleed when we are cut and we would all give our lives for our children.

We are an evolving people. I do wish we were evolving faster. In the meantime, we have to come to this higher consciousness at the speed life has issued us. You might say that the only people that will enjoy this book or find meaning in its pages will be those who already "get it." You could be one who says, "Hey, you're preaching to the choir." Why write a book like this where only like minded people might be the ones who understand the message you are passing along?

Well, let me ask you a question. Have you always been a member of the choir or someone who is in touch with the possibilities in which I write about? Was there not a time or a day that you came to new consciousness and began to see the world and the people in it in a whole new way? We all must come to that place and it is my hope that the insights and reflections I have shared have begun to open the minds and hearts of many who are just beginning to sing. Peace out.

About The Author

Jack Bloomfield is a humanitarian and community builder who is devoted to being a partner in the change necessary for the world to become a place of peace and brotherhood for all people. He is the author of the book, **One Planet United;** *The Problem, The Solution and A Plan of Action* and currently writes a bi-weekly column titled "One Planet United" that has appeared in many assorted publications throughout the state of Florida. The One Planet United column is also forwarded by email to readers across the United States.

Jack is the co-founder and executive director of the non-profit organization, One Planet United Inc. One Planet United's mission states:

"One Planet United is a humanitarian organization that seeks to bring unity and understanding to all people through experiential and educational programs, projects and resources. We are devoted to bring about the elimination of prejudice, intolerance and division, one community at a time."

Jack currently serves as a member of the Coral Springs Interfaith Committee which is a division of the Coral Springs Multi-Cultural Committee and is a past member of the Multi-Cultural Committee of Broward County, Florida. He is a trained hospice volunteer, and the creator of a weekend retreat titled "The Healing Power of Laughter."

He was recently honored as a "Hero of Humanity" by the Art of Living Foundation, a spiritually based educational and service non-profit organization whose programs have benefited over 20,000,000 people worldwide. The foundation presented Jack with the **Sri Sri Ravi Shankar Award for Uplifting Human Values** which is presented annually to community leaders committed to improving the lives of others through their dedication and service to humanity.

Jack has been married to his wife Janice for 30 years and is the proud father of two adult children, Matthew and Jaime.

About One Planet United—
The Organization

One Planet United, a non-profit organization, incorporated in the fall of 2004 and received full tax exempt status 501(c)3 in January of 2005. A portion of the proceeds from the sale of this book will go to help keep the work of One Planet United moving forward.

To learn more about One Planet United, the organization, mission, vision, purpose and more, visit www.opunited.org

Quantity discounts and wholesale information:
For educational and learning institutions, bookstores, wholesalers, and other bulk purchases, quantity discounts for this book are available. Contact One Planet United directly at (954)-340-2115 or email your request to info@opunited.org.

Speaking Engagements/Requests:
Jack is available for speaking engagements at conferences, seminars, corporations, universities and schools. Please contact him directly by email at jack@opunited.org Also, please review the list of speakers on the One Planet United speaker's bureau which can be found by visiting the OPU website.
www.opunited.org

Newsletter/Column:
One Planet United issues a free monthly newsletter as well as a bi-monthly column written by Jack Bloomfield. To receive our newsletter and column, please visit our website at www.opunited.org and type in your e-mail address on the homepage in the space provided.

OPU Store:

One Planet United offers products and resources that help promote the message of our organization. We have a variety of books, CD's, puzzles, tee shirts, coffee mugs, baseball caps, and bumper stickers. Visit www.opunited.org and click on OPU Store.

100% of the proceeds from the sale of OPU products go directly to keeping our mission and vision moving forward.

Fundraising: Many of our products may be purchased at discount prices for fundraising purposes for schools, civic groups and community organizations. Contact us for more information.

The following books have been a part of the inspiration that has led to the creation of this book. I want to thank all of the authors for sharing their wisdom with me and millions of others who are seeking to raise their consciousness to bring about a better world.

Book List

TITLE	AUTHOR
"Mohandas Gandhi" (Essential Writings)	John Dear
"Joshua"	Joseph F. Girzone
"Soul Stories"	Gary Zukav
"A Return to Love"	Marianne Williamson
"World Religions"	John Bowker
"The Sermon on the Mount"	Emmet Fox
"Discovering the Enneagram"	Richard Rohr
"When Religion Becomes Evil"	Charles Kimball
"Tuesdays with Morrie"	Mitch Albom
"Messy Spirituality"	Michael Yaconelli
"Alcoholics Anonymous"	Bill Wilson
"Conversations with God" book 1	Neale Donald Walsch

"A Portrait of Jesus"	Joseph F. Girzone
"A Touch of Wonder"	Arthur Gordon
"A New Christianity for a New World"	John Shelby Spong
"Good Goats. Healing Your Image of God"	Dennis Lynn, Matt Lynn Sheila Fabricant Lynn
"The Lord is My Shepherd"	Harold S. Kushner
"A Second Chance"	Keith Miller
"Further Along the Road Less Traveled"	M. Scott Peck
"How Good Do We Have to Be?"	Harold S. Kushner
"The Seat of the Soul"	Gary Zukav
"Everyday Grace"	Marianne Williamson
"Whispers in the Silence"	John Dennison
"Healing the Shame That Binds You"	John Bradshaw
"The New Revelations"	Neale Donald Walsch
"Belonging: Bonds of Healing And Recovery"	Dennis Linn, Matt Linn, Sheila Fabricant Linn
"Your Money or Your Life"	Joe Dominguez, Vicki Robin
"Never Alone"	Joseph F. Girzone
"The God We Never Knew"	Marcus J. Borg
"Open Mind, Open Heart"	Thomas Keating

"For The Love of God"   Writings by assorted
spiritual teachers

"Kara, the Lonely Falcon"   Joseph F. Girzone

"Self Matters"   Dr. Phil McGraw

"Man's Search for Meaning"   Viktor Frankl

"He Touched Me"   John Powell

"The Grief Recovery Handbook"   John W. James
Frank Cherry

"Getting the Love You Want"   Harville Hendrix

"Homecoming"   John Bradshaw

"The Secret of Staying In Love"   John Powell

"Halftime"   Bob Buford

"Game Plan"   Bob Buford

"Seasons of Your Heart"   Macrina Wiederkehr

"The Power of Now"   Eckhart Tolle

"Beyond Belief"   Elaine Pagels

"Meeting Jesus Again
  For the First Time"   Marcus J. Borg

"What God Wants"   Neale Donald Walsch

"Blessed Unrest"   Paul Hawken

"Becoming Human"   Brian C. Taylor

978-0-595-48798-1
0-595-48798-X

www.ingramcontent.com/pod-product-compliance
Lightning Source LLC
Chambersburg PA
CBHW030312290526
45785CB00001B/316